MASTERING
— T H E —
BASICS

MASTERING
— THE —
BASICS

SIMPLE LESSONS FOR ACHIEVING SUCCESS IN BUSINESS

DEAN KARREL

A POST HILL PRESS BOOK
ISBN: 978-1-64293-209-6
ISBN (eBook): 978-1-64293-210-2

Mastering the Basics:
Simple Lessons for Achieving Success in Business
© 2019 by Dean Karrel
All Rights Reserved

Cover Design by Cody Corcoran

Author Photo by Miho Grant

Post Hill Press
New York • Nashville
posthillpress.com

Published in the United States of America

TABLE OF CONTENTS

INTRODUCTION

No matter what profession you're in or what job you have, there are moments when you question your abilities. It is common to have periods of self-doubt or fear that others are more capable than you are. This is especially true when you start a new job or join a new company.

Early in my career, I experienced this feeling a number of times and, gradually, I learned to work my way through it. Candidly, even today in my work as a career and executive coach, along with being an instructor on LinkedIn Learning, I have occasions when I wonder if I'm making the grade. However, now I've learned to quickly refocus my attention on the skills I have worked so hard to develop. I realize that the person I need to believe in is *me*. That can sometimes be a difficult hurdle to overcome, but it's so important to do so. For me, I realized that focusing on mastering basic skills and adhering to qualities in which I believed would set me apart from others, maximize my abilities, and enable me to successfully achieve my personal goals.

I didn't develop this philosophy overnight, but there were some steps that got me there. I have always been an avid reader of business books, especially ones with quick tips and techniques for ways of doing things better and smarter. I have also benefited from motivational tomes as well, going way back to Norman Vincent Peale's *The Power of Positive Thinking* and Dale Carnegie's *How to Win Friends and Influence People*.

From all of the books I've read, there are seven that have had a profound impact on my thinking and my beliefs in business. They helped change the way I approached situations and gave me confidence to believe I was going in the right direction. You'll recognize a few of these but some others might be a surprise.

While at Prentice-Hall, I became good friends with an author and psychology professor named Dr. Lewis Losoncy. He had written a number of books and many more since but, in 1980, he published *You Can Do It: How to Encourage Yourself.* The book was so basic, yet so clear about methods to be positive, how not to let negative events derail you, and how not to make excuses. Lew's authentic style is one that taught me so much.

There was a time when I would pick up a book at the airport before every business trip. Remember, this was the era before e-books. I collected some good ones like *The Effective Executive* by Peter Drucker and *In Search of Excellence* by Tom Peters and Robert Waterman, Jr. However, there were more than a few that I left in the seat-back pocket on the plane. Then, one day, I grabbed a mass market paperback copy of a book by Robert Townsend called *Up the Organization.* It had been a bestseller many years before, but I had never read it. Townsend was the former CEO of Avis and the subtitle of the book tells it all: *How to Stop the Corporation from Stifling People and Strangling Profits.* As soon as I started reading this book, I was nodding my head in agreement. It is straightforward without business school jargon or theory.

In the middle part of my career, I really questioned whether I was on the right path. My employer was one of the leaders in the industry. There were some brilliant people there and some of them weren't shy about reminding others about it. It could be intimidating at times, to say the least. It was a fast-paced and a highly driven atmosphere that was too much for some people, who left because of that pressure. Over the course of a few years, I reported to a good number of different managers and I always felt that I had to continually prove my abilities. I knew I wasn't being myself.

One day, I picked up Mark McCormack's book, *What They Don't Teach You at Harvard Business School*. These were his notes on being a "street-smart executive" and that you don't need to be a Harvard, Stanford, or Wharton MBA to be successful. In essence, he said that common sense and being yourself is a much more productive and rewarding way to be happy and be an effective businessperson. It's written in an honest and comprehensible style in plain English. This down-to-earth approach is the reason why it sold millions of copies, along with the sequel, *What They Still Don't Teach You at Harvard Business School*.

That book, along with reexamining what I had learned from Gary Gutchell, my first sales manager, about planning, preparation, and believing in yourself changed my thinking of how I wanted to approach my business career going forward. It's interesting how some reflection back to early lessons from Gary and a book by Mark McCormack gave me so much confidence in my own style of getting things done and doing it my way.

The lessons I learned became the philosophy that I would then speak about to the people with whom I worked and the teams I managed.

As my career developed and the companies I worked for grew, I found myself going to more meetings, listening to more presentations, and getting mired in "stuff." One day, I was in a bookstore and I spotted a book by Jack Trout with a title that caught my eye, *The Power of Simplicity: A Management Guide to Cutting Through the Nonsense and Doing Things Right*. I knew about Jack since he had written a marketing bestseller with Al Ries called *Positioning*. Again, I was nodding my head in agreement as he explained how to get rid of complexity, keep things focused, and embrace simplicity. This is something I have tried to follow in both business and my personal life.

I think Patrick Lencioni's *The Five Dysfunctions of a Team* should be required reading for anyone in business. It's a short leadership fable that, in less than two hundred pages, teaches some important lessons about working with others within your organization. The five dysfunctions are a part of a model that includes: The Absence of Trust, The Fear of Conflict, The Lack of Commitment, The Avoidance of Accountability, and The Inattention to Results. These powerful messages are taught in a non-theoretical way through a real-life example in the fable. When I first met Patrick, he told me that this book would sell a million copies. Being the savvy sales manager, I tried to tone down his enthusiasm by saying that most books rarely sell more than ten thousand units. Over the next thirty minutes I learned first-hand about The Five Dysfunctions, especially conflict. Patrick and his team's efforts have resulted in millions of copies of this book being sold! It is a fantastic book with an outstanding message.

The Leadership Challenge by James Kouzes and Barry Posner is another bestselling book, part of a franchise of products to help inspire better leaders. Their Leadership Practices Inventory 360 assessment tool needs to be on your list of required assignments. The five practices to exemplary leadership are: Model the Way, Inspire a Shared Vision, Challenge the Process, Enable others to Act, and Encourage the Heart. By reading this book, taking the assessment, and following their guidance, I know I've become a better leader. "Encouraging the Heart" is one of great focus for me because I believe rewarding and recognizing others is so critically important. It is something I have tried diligently to practice. (*Lead from the Heart* by Mark Crowley is another outstanding book on the subject.)

The concepts from these books and lessons I learned from great leaders I worked with through the years formed who I am today. And I believe I'm a work in progress, as lifelong learning and continuous improvement is something that I feel is essential.

The focus on learning essential business skills, developing your confidence, being a good person, and recognizing the priorities in our lives is what *Mastering the Basics* is all about. We all can't be the top performer in school or the senior executive of the company, so you need to figure out what steps you can take to be more successful. You won't find all of the answers in this book, but my goal is to inspire you to look at your job, colleagues, and employer differently. The topics in this book are a part of my philosophy on how to be a better businessperson and individual.

DEAN'S PHILOSOPHY

● ● ●

Through the years, I have tried to focus on some simple principles and values that I believe are essential. These are strategies that I follow and have taught to both colleagues and my children. It doesn't matter if you've got a fancy job title or a degree from an Ivy League university. If you are unable to understand the critical nature of these basic skills, you will limit your potential.

Are these groundbreaking? No, but they align with my view that, by mastering simple concepts, you can be successful as well as a better person. There is more to each one than just the few words listed. Think about the impact of a smile or a note, the importance of integrity, and recognizing what really matters in life.

1. Be Good to People
2. Smile and Say Hello
3. Have a Good Work Ethic
4. Send Thank You Notes
5. Always Be Learning—Lifelong Learning
6. Confidence—Believe in Yourself
7. Integrity and Character
8. Be Authentic, Be Genuine
9. Planning and Preparation
10. Know Your Priorities, Family Comes First, and Focus on What Really Matters

ADMIT WHEN YOU ARE WRONG AND APOLOGIZE IF NECESSARY

● ● ●

How many times have you watched the news on television and a story comes on about a businessperson or politician who is suspected of doing something wrong? This person expresses some outrage and then gives a long-winded denial. A few days later when more details come out, the person hems and haws, admits there may have been some mistakes made but he or she neglects to say, "I'm sorry." Then, weeks later, when the matter has become a full-blown scandal, the person tearfully says, "I apologize."

Now, this is an extreme example and I hope you never encounter a situation where you've got TV cameras and reporters with microphones in your face. However, there are often times when we do make a mistake in business. The fact is many great innovations have been developed, new products created, and important issues solved because a number of missteps and mistakes were made beforehand. Trial and error are a fundamental way of solving problems in science and in business.

However, when a mistake is made, the smartest thing to do is to flag it early, make your manager aware and, if necessary, apologize sooner rather than later. This way, you can get assistance along with support to correct the situation and get things back on the right track.

There have been times in my career when a "concerned" or "angry" customer has called me or had been transferred to me. Early in my career, I would try to explain what happened, give a detailed view of what transpired and then finally apologize. However, over time, I realized that people don't want to hear "why;" they want to hear "how" we plan to solve the problem. I've disarmed many heated voices on the other end of the telephone by letting them vent and then saying, "You're right, we were wrong. I take full responsibility and I sincerely apologize. This is how I'd like to fix it." You would be amazed at how the person's tone immediately changes, and you can almost sense surprise or shock on the other end of the telephone.

A truly successful business professional is the one who raises his or her hand and admits when something has gone wrong. These people ask for assistance, cut their losses, and just apologize. It's always the smart approach, so the sooner you do it, the better off you'll be. Just take a deep breath and get it done. Frankly, this advice holds true in business, or with a friend, your partner, or your spouse.

AGE IS A VERY
SENSITIVE SUBJECT

● ● ●

Can you think of a situation in a business setting when anything positive can come up when the subject turns to someone's age? No, because there rarely is.

Even if you're discussing something in a casual or seemingly harmless fashion, the numbers will either be too low, too high, off by ten years, or just overall insulting. I remember when I was in my early twenties, I looked even younger and, when I would call on a customer, I would often hear, "Are you right out of college?" People would chuckle and say, "Oh, you'll appreciate it when you're older." I've also known people who've lost hair early or had a more mature look and people would totally misjudge their age. It seems like an innocent mistake, but many people feel insulted by the incorrect references.

Also, depending on your ethnicity or culture, bringing up someone's age also could lead you right into a hornet's nest of a potential legal matter of age discrimination. Making a broad generalization about a group of people, whether millennials or baby-boomers is likely to earn you a trip to the human resources department.

In all business settings, as well as your personal life, steer clear of discussions about age. Nine times out of ten, you'll be wrong and, unfortunately, people don't forget those kinds of comments.

ALWAYS BE LEARNING—THE BENEFITS OF BEING A LIFELONG LEARNER

● ● ●

So, you graduated from high school, then went to college and received a degree or maybe even earned a master's degree or a doctorate. Perhaps, you went to a trade school or got a certificate with some training in a specialized field. Does that mean the process of furthering your education has now ended? Of course not, but you will find a wide range of opportunities for lifelong learning after you've completed the traditional school options.

For years, medical researchers have said that reading books, taking classes, researching online, and continuing with educating ourselves is very important for keeping our brains stimulated and healthy. There are many studies about that, but I'm particularly focused on the process of continuing to learn new ideas so you can become better at business and in your personal life. There are so many ways to always be learning and, in some cases, it's free or low-cost. Lifelong learning and the process of continuing to enhance and develop our skills is something we should regularly monitor to ensure that we have a plan in place for accomplishing it.

The next few entries are some ideas for you to consider.

ALWAYS BE LEARNING—BOOKS, MAGAZINES, AND ONLINE RESOURCES

● ● ●

I've always felt that an investment in a book pays dividends. Along with keeping your mind fresh for less than twenty dollars, if you pick up four or five new ideas, then that's a great payback. There's always a list posted somewhere online of the best new books or ones recommended by other avid readers. You can scroll through subject listings at your online store or do it the old-fashioned way with a trip to your local bookstore.

Did I really say magazines? This world has certainly changed dramatically over the past decade, but in certain categories, the readership is still healthy online. I read *Inc.* and *Fast Company* online and always find an article or two with some great ideas or thoughts about a topic I hadn't considered before. Go online and check out *Forbes, Wired,* and *Bloomberg* and I bet you'll be pleasantly surprised.

While you're online, visit your industry's websites or associations. Some provide some great content that's customized specifically for your business. The human resources, training, and educational fields come to mind. Check sites like TheMuse.com, Entrepreneur.com and Inc.com.

I'm a big fan of following influencers on LinkedIn. People like Travis Bradberry, Jill Schlesinger, Betty Liu, and Sir

Richard Branson are just a few on my list. They post some great thinking about a variety of different subjects.

Where else? Here's a great networking idea: ask a few peers or contacts from other companies. What can be easier than asking, "What are you reading to stay on top of things?"

ALWAYS BE LEARNING— COLLEGE AND UNIVERSITY CLASSES

• • •

When I decided to leave my job in the corporate world, I went back to college to take classes in career and executive coaching. I had years of practical experience, but I lacked the foundational skills, along with some type of official certification. I can't tell you enough about what a great experience these classes were. The energy in the classroom was contagious. I was networking with a new group of people, and I was realizing how much more I can still learn.

Taking courses at night or on the weekends is a pretty big commitment. We must have time with our families and, also, time to just relax. However, I'd recommend you seriously consider it if you can allocate some free time during the year. Check with your human resources department, as many companies have tuition reimbursement programs when you take classes that will enhance your professional skills.

The other possibility is to take a course online at home. It's much easier from a scheduling point of view, but you do miss out on the face-to-face interaction and opportunities for other conversations. There's also the issue of finding quiet time at home without distractions. However, for some courses, such as technology classes, doing them online does make a lot of sense.

Keep your eye out for continuing education classes, since those are less costly, and you can often complete them in a few weeks, rather than the two or three months for a course taken at a college. If you live near any college or university, get on its mailing list to take advantage of guest lectures and special events.

Taking a course for a full semester is a major commitment but I'd highly recommend doing so if you can swing it. By the way, I'm continuing to enroll in classes at New York University.

ALWAYS BE LEARNING—LINKEDIN LEARNING

● ● ●

Online learning through video-based courses has come a long way. Years ago, many of these classes were poorly produced and, hence, tough to watch. The content was adequate, but far from top-notch. That's no longer the case, and you're missing a major learning opportunity if you don't seriously explore taking some classes this way.

I've been a fan of LinkedIn Learning (previously called Lynda.com) for a while. (Full disclosure—I now have a few of my own courses on the site too, so I am a bit biased). That said, what a great way to take courses at your own pace with instructors who are specialists in their fields. There are some excellent courses available and I think it is well worth your time to investigate them more. Many companies, local libraries, or the college you attend may provide you with free access. If not, LinkedIn Learning often has a free trial offer or you can sign up for about twenty-five dollars a month.

There are other great sites you should also investigate such as Coursera, Udemy, Udacity, Khan Academy, Skillsoft, CrossKnowledge, Brainshark, ITProTV, and many others. Some are focused on specific disciplines, while others are at a different skillset level. They all enable you to learn something new, on your own schedule, where you want, and in my mind, for a bargain. I think this is a great investment in yourself.

ALWAYS BE LEARNING— SEMINARS, WEBINARS, MICROLEARNING

● ● ●

Sometimes we just don't have the time for courses in the evening at a university or can't commit to a week at some school for an intensive program. So here are some other options to consider.

I love the quick online approach of a webinar. Some are free and some are hooks to get you to buy a fee-based service, so just make sure you know that you may get some heavy-duty pitching for other courses. I'd advise getting some recommendations, too, if the webinar has been offered before. It's really not a bad way to learn something at your own pace online. The old-fashioned webinar is the in-person seminar. You should keep your eyes open for these when they are linked to industry conventions or are offered through professional associations.

These are all ways of getting information and learning new skills in small doses. Thus, the phrase in the learning and development community called microlearning. It is that direct in its meaning. You're learning a specific new skill, or being trained on a new way of doing things, in a more focused and shorter period of time. It's a great way of cutting right to the chase, not wasting time, getting precise information, and in many cases, customized to the needs of you or your small group.

With each of these options, the learning is very focused, intense, and of short duration.

ALWAYS BE LEARNING— YOUR COMPANY'S LEARNING & DEVELOPMENT DEPARTMENT

• • •

Many companies have in-house programs and classes offered through the human resources department or in larger employers, a learning and development department. These offerings can cover a variety of topics from leadership development to training on new software. You'll find details through internal communication methods or on corporate portals. For some programs, you may need to be nominated. But it never hurts to raise your hand and ask. Some companies even have informal lunchtime sessions with a special speaker covering a subject or panel assembled to discuss a certain topic. I could really kick myself for not taking advantage of these opportunities more often through the years.

The learning and development staff or corporate trainers, or whatever they're labeled, are eager to work with people within your company. Reach out and let them know some of the areas where you would like to learn more and gain additional skills. I guarantee you'll be pleasantly surprised at how much they want to support you.

Your own company can be a great source for learning new skills. Don't let this free opportunity to enhance your skills go to waste. Take advantage of these offerings.

ALWAYS BE LEARNING— PERSONAL EDUCATIONAL TRAINING BUDGET

• • •

We have budgets for our expenses that cover pretty much everything, such as electricity, mortgage, or rent costs, food, entertainment like Netflix and internet access, and, hopefully, we tuck money away for vacations. Why don't you set up a personal educational training budget, too? Set aside some funds with each paycheck. Then, as it grows, maybe you use it to take that class? Sign for the online certification program? Join LinkedIn Learning?

Invest in yourself, since there is always something new to learn and ways for us to improve. Educating ourselves never stops, but you have to take the initiative to get started.

ASK FOLLOW-UP QUESTIONS

• • •

How many times have you left a meeting, heard a presentation, or had a conversation with someone and, after you left, wished you had asked a question or two about something that was said? There are a variety of reasons why this happens and it's something that we all should work to improve.

Sometimes, we feel intimidated or fearful of looking ignorant or we're embarrassed by asking a question to which you assume everyone else knows the answer. I smile sometimes when a speaker says, "Does everyone know what I mean by that?" People sit there, avert their eyes from the speaker, or nod their head in agreement. I can guarantee that one quarter of the attendees has no idea. Now, when I'm asked a question, I take a deep breath and just say, "I don't know." The worst that can happen is that the response simply confirms what I may have thought something meant.

Asking follow-up questions also shows your interest in the speaker or the colleague with whom you're speaking. It's a way for him or her to add more detail and clarification to the subject.

When you ask questions, you're making sure what you heard was accurate. This would be especially important if the discussion may be somewhat controversial. "You said 'X;' is that what you really meant? Maybe you can phrase it another way?" Or it may involve a topic of significance for your company and you want to be sure the information you heard is accurate. "I want to clarify that our expense budgets will be reduced by what percentage?"

Follow-up questions are used to clarify, show interest, and reconfirm. They're not intended to derail a meeting or serve as a cross examination much like a court room. Good questioning serves many purposes and savvy businesspeople aren't shy about asking when they need to know more.

ASSESSMENT TESTS

● ● ●

There are many types of assessment tests used by employers for a variety of purposes. I don't know about you, but hearing the word "test" always made my shoulders tense up and stomach tighten with memories of a college exam that I was probably ill-prepared to take. The other issue with testing is that we assume we're being graded.

In business, an assessment test is really an evaluation used to review your abilities, how others may perceive you, or flag areas in which you need improvement. If you take them with an open mind and answer the questions honestly, they can be very powerful tools to help you be a more effective and successful business professional.

There are employment tests and personality tests commonly used by Human Resources departments when applicants are being reviewed for open positions. There are career aptitude assessments that give guidance and ideas on what direction you might want to consider for a career development plan.

However, once you have a few years under your belt in your job and are looking to advance to the next level or enhance your skills, there are some assessments that I recommend highly.

Management and Leadership assessments are pretty straightforward analyses of how we're either performing currently or how we would perform in a new leadership role. There are personality tests distinct from those used during the hiring process which examine whether you work with others or how your style fits in an organization. I'm a big fan of emotional intelligence tests and I've seen many people surprised with the feedback they receive. It can be such a productive and valuable eye-opener.

Ask your human resources department what assessments are available for employees. There are also many free ones you can take online and others that are modestly priced. The more you can learn about yourself in business settings, the better able you'll be to enhance your skills. Take advantage of the opportunity to take these assessments when they are offered.

AT THE END OF THE DAY, IT IS A BUSINESS

● ● ●

Whether we work for a large global corporation, a small business of ten employees, or a non-profit organization, at the end of the day, the company writing our paycheck has a mission or goal.

Whether it's maximizing revenue and profits or seeking grants and soliciting more donations, as staff members or employees, we have a job: to work hard to achieve the objectives of our company.

That's a real cut-and-dry way of looking at things, but it is true. We can have a great office location, fun colleagues, and a nice set of perks, but if our company isn't fulfilling its mission or making the necessary profit, then keeping the business afloat isn't sustainable.

There are matters of culture, the leadership we follow, compensation, and work fulfillment that are the key ingredients of whether we like our job or not, but all that being said, we still are all just one piece of the puzzle.

Public companies have an obligation to their shareholders and private companies to their owners. It's a business and the objective for them is to be successful and make money. As employees, we are key ingredients to make this possible, while at the same time, if we're not meeting their expectations, they can and will make changes.

Companies do want a positive culture and happy teams, but you can never forget that, at the end of the day, leadership can and will make difficult decisions to make the business improve.

BE A CHAMPION

• • •

To me, a champion is someone within your company who is a vocal supporter of a project being developed, a brand being marketed, or an initiative that is underway. They may not be the leader or the owner, but their voice and support carry a lot of weight.

An example for me would be when my former employer was looking to potentially expand the use of the Salesforce CRM. It was a major expense and there were some upper-level executives of the company who were concerned about usage and the return on investment. Thankfully, there were some champions from sales, marketing, business development, and even the finance team who spoke up and helped generate positive momentum to accomplish the expanded implementation.

Are you paid for being a champion? Well, not directly, but the influence you exert will make a difference within your company and, more often than not, with your career. In my mind, genuine and sincere champions are leaders. When you see something that makes sense to support and it can help your department or company in a positive way, don't sit back. Step up and be a champion.

BE AN EVANGELIST

● ● ●

An evangelist in the business world is someone who helps spread word about your product, your service, your company, or anything else you may be trying to promote. Evangelists are found both within your organization and outside of it, but I think they're even more effective when they are buyers, consumers, or current users of your company's offering.

Apple is probably one of the best examples of a company with evangelists supporting its products. For years, Apple's customers who buy Macs, iPads, and iPhones become marketing arms for the company.

For me, it comes back to this principle: if you think something is valuable, can be of value to someone else, or can help people do their work better, speak up and tell everyone about it. Be an evangelist and let others benefit from what you've experienced or learned.

BE AN INFLUENCER

● ● ●

When you hear the word "Influencer," you're probably thinking of celebrities who have millions of followers on Facebook, Instagram, Twitter, or other social media outlets. On LinkedIn, names like Jeff Weiner, Meg Whitman, Charlene Li, and Mark Cuban come to mind.

However, your views and your opinions can and do matter to everyone from the person next to your work station, a customer you might speak with on the telephone, or someone who reads an article you've posted.

To influence means that you can change someone's thinking, are able to alter his behavior, or have an impact on his beliefs. At a minimum, it's the ability to get people to think more by opening their minds to new ideas. It is a very powerful skill that good leaders have. However, you can be an influencer even if you're an entry-level employee or don't have a title of manager, director, or vice president. It's having the confidence to express your views when you believe it's important for others to hear you or read your thoughts.

Remember, though, while your ego might enjoy having thousands of fans or followers, you need to focus on your message. The ability to impact others and make a difference with your targeted audience, whether it's a handful of colleagues or thousands in your industry, is the sign of a leader and a true influencer.

BE AUTHENTIC

● ● ●

You know those people who seem to act differently depending on the setting or environment they're in? They might put on a show of authority in a group meeting, or seem aloof when they don't want to get involved with a team project, or gloat when they've had success just to make sure everyone is aware about it.

When you start off working or get a new job, you sometimes get advice from people who say you need to be more outgoing, more aggressive, or extroverted, and so on. Some may say that you need to have the personality of the stereotype of that job. Well, what does that mean?

I'm here to tell you that you don't need to change your style or your personality. What you need to be is yourself, be real and be authentic, because that's who you are. We can all improve our qualities and skills but, deep down, we really can't change who we are without risking being a phony. For me, being authentic boils down to three qualities—vulnerability, character, and transparency.

Being authentic means you're just being who you are and not trying to change yourself based on your colleagues or with whom you're meeting. It's showing your positive skills, while at the same time, not being afraid of letting others see your weaknesses, areas where you may need to improve, and even exhibiting a dose of vulnerability.

All of this closely ties into your character, which is what I feel is the true substance of an individual. Being true to yourself, real, and authentic are not just qualities important to being a successful salesperson or business leader, but an individual too. Our character is how people perceive us, trust us, and want to work with us or be around us. There are many great quotes about character but one of my favorites is from John Wooden, the famed college basketball coach, who said, "Be more concerned with your character than your reputation, because your character is what you really are, while your reputation is merely what others think you are."

People who are authentic and real are admired for being transparent. Colleagues, peers, and customers don't have to worry about trying to figure out what open and authentic people are really saying. They are respected and trusted for their honesty; people often say about them, "What you see is what you get." Isn't that much better than being someone who your colleagues don't believe or your clients don't respect?

In business, we need to be transparent and real. If we're perceived as someone who is hard to figure out or someone who may be embellishing a statement, then we run the risk of being unapproachable or, worse yet, untrustworthy.

Frankly, it gets too complicated to try to be someone you're not, so keep things simple; just be yourself and be true to your character. You'll find that others will respect you, admire you, and when you move to leadership roles, they will follow you.

BE CAREFUL WITH YOUR ONLINE POSTS

● ● ●

There are so many social networking sites from Facebook to LinkedIn to Instagram to YouTube and whatever new ones that seem to crop up regularly. It's really pretty amazing the reach you can attain and the impact you can make for yourself or the business you're supporting.

However, for all the positive, there are some negatives to watch out for. The big one being, once we post something and it's out there, it's really difficult to reel it back in.

As businesspeople, we want our clients and customers focused on our product or service. The last thing we need is their attention diverted to other issues or topics that may be offensive to them and create a negative feeling about us or our company. When you're posting your opinions, ask yourself whether you're overstepping your bounds with non-business discussions within your business network.

We all have friends or coworkers who sometimes post political or other personal commentary on social media sites. There's nothing wrong with that, but you need to be careful about what you post, what you say, and, more importantly, how vehemently you express yourself. I've had a few friends, acquaintances from other companies and even coworkers, make comments online that prompted me to say, "Wow, I didn't know that about them." Then I'll say, "I didn't want to know that about them!" Are you nodding your head in agreement as you read this?

Political leanings, religious beliefs, and feelings about social issues are hot buttons in the news every day. Each of us has views which are very personal and our own. Mixing them with business is very, very dangerous and can have a direct impact on your career. Someone who sees one of your posts can cancel your next sales appointment or choose not to interview you for an opening for which you had applied. Before posting, weigh the upside and downside of having your views seen by everyone.

Again, there's nothing wrong with sharing your opinion, but, as business professionals, we need to be cautious about the ramifications. Let your views sit for a while in your thinking before you post them somewhere. Stepping back, evaluating the consequences, or just taking a deep breath before posting some political comment is well worth the pause.

BE FAIR

● ● ●

This is a more difficult concept to explain. I think you all probably know what I mean by "being fair." In fact, it's covered somewhat in other entries such as, Be Good to People with Whom You Work.

However, it's more than that, and I believe the words, "Be Fair" carry a lot of weight. Along with being good to others, I can think of a few other qualities that tie into being fair. When you're fair, you show respect, understanding, thoughtfulness, and treat people equally. I also feel that truly listening to others plays into this, along with being a role model and a leader to all and not showing favorites.

In one sentence, for me, being fair comes down to being a decent, caring, and honorable human being. That's clear to me, but I encourage you to reflect on what being fair means to you. What else comes to mind? How would you evaluate yourself? Can you improve? There will be a point when you nod your head and know clearly what it means for you to be fair.

BE GOOD TO PEOPLE
WITH WHOM
YOU WORK

● ● ●

We've all heard stories, positive and negative, about how people feel they are treated at work. I'm sure we also all have our own personal stories from the companies where we have worked and colleagues with whom we have interacted. I think being nice to people at work also ties in with corporate culture, the skills with or lack thereof for emotional intelligence, and the basic ability to have empathy for others when they need our support.

The act of caring and supporting others we work with is one the five key practices in Jim Kouzes and Barry Posner's bestselling book, *The Leadership Challenge*. They call it, "Encouraging the Heart," and they show how powerful it can be when you are rewarding, recognizing, and encouraging others around you. There's another excellent book on the subject that I recommend—Mark Crowley's *Lead From the Heart*. Being nice at work and its impact on corporate culture is something that's important to me. I have been fortunate to have worked with some terrific companies in my career. I have seen how a positive and supportive culture can drive teamwork and outstanding results. More often than not, the most successful companies are the ones where culture is highly valued and recognized by colleagues at all levels of the organization.

So, does that mean we need to always be cheering people on, never criticizing, and always having a happy face on? Of course not. In fact, honesty, directness, and even a dose of conflict is needed for companies to succeed. Some people just "get it," and know the value of being supportive to others and being a trusted, valued, and "good" coworker. Those are the people with whom I want to align myself. So, give it a try, focus more on being nicer to people at work. It will make you and your coworkers feel better and I'm sure you'll be paid back in many positive ways!

BE OPEN TO
CONSTRUCTIVE
CRITICISM

• • •

When you ask for constructive criticism, often, you don't really want it. You may say, say, "Yes, please give me your feedback, good and bad, as I'd love to hear it." But if you hear even the slightest bit of criticism, your eyebrows furrow, you go into defensive mode, and you're ready to respond with a sharp-tongued comment.

Some people are better than this than others and I've improved a lot over the years, but candidly, I can still feel my shoulders tighten up a bit when I get feedback not to my full liking. Remember, I'm talking about constructive criticism. If someone is downright rude and criticizing you, then you need to use your skills of just not listening or walking away.

When you ask for feedback, remember you're doing so for positive reasons. You want to personally improve or the project you're showing to be better represented. So, if the news is not to your liking, stop, take a breath, and just listen. Don't exhibit any non-verbal communication. After the person finishes, think about some good qualifying questions you can ask. Maybe the person can provide greater details that will make it easier for you to accept the feedback. You also need to take into account the source of the constructive criticism. Frankly, it is the job of your manager or other higher-level supervisor to give you feedback. If they don't, then they're really doing a disservice to you and the employer. Constructive criticisms are suggestions to help you improve. We all need to view them as positive interactions with someone who wants to assist us to get to a better place. If we view them in defensive way, then we are only hurting ourselves.

BE RELIABLE

• • •

In my view, being reliable is so critical and one of those qualities that's on the short list of things that separates the very best people from all of the rest. Some people may say this word is interchangeable with "dependable" but I'm focusing on reliable here.

In business, there are many examples of actions that exhibit your reliability. For some, it just comes as second nature. However, when you have a colleague, peer, manager, or direct report who has this trait, the person is likely to be valued and appreciated. These are people whom we can never take for granted.

Here are a few situations that come to mind. Reliable people keep promises, and if they say they're going to be prepared for a meeting, they are. If their part of the team project is needed by Friday, it's ready by then. They don't offer excuses, they don't complain, and they just get things done without any drama or issues.

As a manager, the direct reports who are reliable are appreciated since they provide stability, they're trusted, and can be counted on. If your manager says that you are one of those people, that's a real compliment and you should feel pretty good about yourself.

BE VULNERABLE

● ● ●

Over the course of my career, I've spoken in front of hundreds of people. The audiences were either salespeople, other colleagues from my company, or, in one case, more than five hundred technology representatives from a company we all know well. Inevitably, at some point, someone will ask if I ever get nervous speaking in front of large groups after all these years. I smile, nod my head, and say, "You're darn right, I do!" I may be a bit nervous, but I'm not scared, because I'm well prepared and I'm confident in my skills.

The reaction is generally always the same. The person's eyes widen, and he or she says, "Wow, really?" I can then sense that I've created a positive connection with that person. Vulnerability breaks down barriers, shows that you're genuine, which aligns closely with being authentic. Showing your vulnerability is a great equalizer and some of the best leaders use it to motivate their teams and enhance the connection with their coworkers.

Do you have any business colleagues or friends who always seem to have a wall around them and it's really difficult to know what they're thinking? They'll look at you and give a disinterested nod, or worse yet, have no visible reaction and just stare into your eyes. Do you trust them? Do you feel confident in being open around them? Keeping a focused, non-emotional face with a monotone speech pattern can sometimes be a very effective strategy. As a salesperson, some of the best buyers I've met have mastered that skill.

However, what I am talking about are the day-to-day issues, highlights, successes, disappointments, and the obstacles we face in our careers and jobs, whether we are an entry-level salesperson or a vice-president of sales. I'm a firm believer that it's perfectly acceptable for you to express your feelings, letting your guard down every so often about the highs and the lows of what we do and letting people see your vulnerable side.

There was a time in my career when I doubted some of my abilities. Even though I had been well trained and had a successful track record, I was not feeling good about what I was doing and the direction in which I was headed. Through the years, I've had no problem telling other colleagues I've worked with stories like that and showing a bit of my vulnerable side. I see it as a great way to make the human connection with people, and I use it as training technique.

However, vulnerability is not to be linked with being defeated. Letting your emotions be seen—and even some of your flaws—is a good quality, but it needs to be balanced by showing drive, work ethic, and the confidence that you can rebound.

This openness and sharing of our feelings are a positive way of showing our vulnerability. In fact, the most confident people are the ones who let others see and hear their inner feelings. There's nothing wrong with saying we're a bit unsure of what to do, that we may question whether we're making the right decisions, or that we're a bit confused. We believe in people and often follow leaders who break down barriers and let us see them as they are. You build trust and loyalty when you show your human side so don't be afraid to let people see that in you.

BEING POSITIVE
IS A CHOICE

● ● ●

M ost of us would probably agree that it's more fun to work with people who are positive, upbeat, and are striving for success. Someone who greets you with a nice warm smile or congratulates you sincerely after you get some good news is certainly the type of individual I'd prefer as a colleague.

Those who are pessimistic or always negative can drag everyone down. They're the ones who groan going into a meeting, slump in their chair when someone is speaking, and always bring up the reasons why something won't work.

For me, having a positive outlook ties into believing in yourself, being confident, and also encouraging and supporting others to be successful and upbeat too. It's having an attitude of not letting negative situations set you back.

Being positive just doesn't happen by saying, "I'm going to be positive." You have to work at it, you have to find ways to get the negative things out of your life and align yourself with people who want do good things and be better too. In business, we want people to see our enthusiasm and hear the positive tone in our voice in all our interactions.

I think it's also recognizing that every day isn't going to be a sunny day either. There's a balance to all of this too. You need to realize you can't be upbeat and positive all of the time. Just as there are people who always seem to find the negative in everything there are those who seem to overdo it with their smiles, greetings, back-slapping, and, "Life is just great!" reactions.

We've all had times in our lives when maybe we weren't the brightest ray of sunshine, our confidence was at a low point, or we weren't the person waving our arms saying, "Follow me." Getting stuck in those ruts is not ideal, which is why it's also so important to encourage and support others when we see them needing a positive jolt from us.

Your attitude needs to be strong and upbeat not just when things are going well, but how you react when things aren't perfect as well—it is during those times people will judge you on how you react. Ever work with people who are so happy, friendly, and positive in good times, but show a nasty, negative, and competitive side in more difficult situations? You don't want to be that person.

To be clear, I'm not saying we can, or always should be, happy. But being positive is a choice, and more often than not, success follows those who are realistic, yet always remain positive. Positive people are leaders. They have everyone join in and celebrate the good news in our personal lives and in business situations. The best businesspeople find ways of guiding and supporting people through turbulent times or when that hill seems too big to climb. That choice to be a positive person is in your hands.

BODY LANGUAGE

● ● ●

Non-verbal communication is, in many ways, as important as verbal communication. It's amazing what you can learn about people just by watching them. You can tell if they're happy, annoyed, bored, interested, or angry, just to name just a few emotions. I'm one of those lousy poker players because the other players always know what I'm thinking. That's not a good thing either, since it often conveys a message that I really don't want expressed. Body language can be improved if need be, but it requires you to recognize its importance and then spending time to alter any bad habits you may have.

For the next few entries, I'm going to focus on some common body language examples, such as posture and the use of our hands and arms. I'm also going to look at two more specific ones with eye contact and smiling, since they are real trigger points for me when I meet people. There are articles on this subject and even books written about the importance of body language and non-verbal communication. I think it's worth your investment in time to learn more about it.

In business, we are evaluated, reviewed, and, as we all know, judged in many ways from the people we meet and the people we work with every day. It could be by the products or services we represent, the company we work for, how we write or speak, and also by our non-verbal actions too. Recognizing the impact that body language has on how we're perceived is critical for us to understand and take the necessary steps to continually improve.

BODY LANGUAGE—
EYE CONTACT

• • •

How many times have you met someone who never looks you in the eyes? It seems as if they are looking over your shoulder, at the wall beside you, the photos on your desk, their feet, or just have that blank dumb stare off into the distance.

When I'm with this person, I start wondering if I'm boring him or whether he's looking for someone more interesting with whom to have a conversation. Can someone be that rude and not look directly at me?

Through the years I have learned that we ignore mentioning this concern to colleagues who have this issue. Frankly, we really should be giving them the heads-up rather than just letting it be. For some, they just don't know that their eye contact is so poor, for others it is an inner shyness or fear of close communication, and for some, I think it actually is a bit of arrogance.

So, the heck with the arrogant folks since they won't change anyway, but pass along this tip to the others.

Poor eye contact is a very hard habit to break, but the advice I always give people is that you have to practice changing your mannerisms. When you're alone, find a mirror and just start talking and looking at yourself. (That's best done when no one is home, since friends and family members will think you have more than just an eye contact issue.) The other method is to practice at your desk and turn on your webcam doing the same exercise.

Frankly, it can be like torture to do this and don't worry if you feel self-conscious, because it's perfectly normal. However, what you'll notice is that you do dart your eyes, you do have trouble having eye contact for more than ten seconds, but in time, you'll get more and more comfortable. Talk about your work, your successes, and concentrate until your eyes don't stray.

It can be painful, but the practice does work. In my view, giving eye contact is a basic sign of respect and neglecting it can show signs of lack of confidence, indifference, or arrogance.

BODY LANGUAGE—SMILE

● ● ●

You wouldn't think I'd have to include the importance of a smile in a book about how to master basic skills. Really, how difficult can it be to show a smile when you meet someone new or have a positive reaction to something? A smile is an easy way to start a new conversation with a person you just met, as it breaks down a barrier and cuts through any initial tension. It's also a very simple non-verbal way of expressing gratitude, acceptance, or support. Unfortunately, I do have to include this entry in the book because I have met so many people who just don't recognize the importance of a smile.

I'm convinced there's a significant number of people who must keep a lemon handy to suck on before going into a meeting room, stepping into a gathering of new acquaintances, or even walking the aisles of a supermarket (probably to buy more lemons).

Over the course of my career, the smile (or lack thereof) from buyers, new colleagues, or job candidates that I've met has made for some difficult first impressions for me. Candidly, I just don't understand why for some people this is such a hard thing, like it is a task, or sign of weakness to show a smile.

Of course, having said that, there's nothing worse than a fake smile, since you then look cynical or sarcastic. You need to be genuine and show some positive expression of wanting to meet someone. Do the mirror test again. Look at yourself in a mirror with and without a smile. Did you know you looked that unfriendly when there was no expression? I guarantee you'll get and hear positive feedback when you make a better attempt to smile from now on.

BODY LANGUAGE— POSTURE

● ● ●

We can look at posture in two ways. One would be how we appear when we're standing or walking and the other would be how we look when we're sitting at our desk or at conference table with others.

How I stand has actually been a lifelong issue for me. In fact, I can still remember a second-grade teacher sternly telling me to, "Stand up straight" and then having me practice that by balancing a book on my head. That didn't solve the issue of my posture and it also proved that knowledge can't be transferred to your brain that way either. It really comes down to recognizing the problem and reminding ourselves to "Stand up straight." That said, I've still had occasions when I was given friendly reminders by thoughtful colleagues that I had that "tired" look.

How we sit at our desks has actually been examined a lot and is something that we can and should proactively work to improve. There are times when we've all fallen into habit of leaning over toward our computer or slumping down in our chairs as we type away. Not only do we look bad, it's bad for our health too. There are some great solutions, from ergonomic tips for better sitting, to more modern chairs, and to standing desks. This is worth your investment in time to find a better set-up for yourself.

Your posture in meetings can really show how poor body language can cause others to perceive you in a bad way. I think you can learn a lot about people with how they sit in a group meeting at the conference table. We've all seen them. The person stretched out at a forty-five-degree angle, the one with his hand draped over the back of his chair, or the woman tapping her foot as she sits there, seemingly impatiently.

Next time you go to meeting in a conference room, take a second to think about how you look sitting there. Are you interested? Slumped over a bit? Is your head resting in the palm off your hand? The body language of posture can speak volumes and, unfortunately, oftentimes coveys a negative message, so it's worth thinking about to ensure you're at your best.

BODY LANGUAGE— GESTURES AND THE USE OF OUR ARMS AND HANDS

● ● ●

These are pretty obvious body language signals, since we've all seen the coworkers with their head in their hands, the one tugging at their ear lobe, or the one tapping their fingers on the table. The gestures we spot with various moments and positions of hands and arms, along with what they could mean, cover the gamut.

It's always interesting to watch the meeting where some difficult discussions take place and you see one or two colleagues cross their arms over their chest. If that's not a give-a-way of someone getting angry or defensive, I don't know what is. Those people sit there and then you'll see them take a deep breath and go into a two-minute speech why the other person's comments are wrong or the incorrect conclusions are being made. Through the years, I've seen some pretty high-level people cross their arms and it was a telltale sign to duck. You would have thought they might have been coached to flag it for correction, but it never happened.

The reality is: from crossed legs to nail biting and from our head tilted to the side to rubbing our hands, everything conveys or could be construed to convey some meaning. Pay some attention to how you sit or may appear in a business setting. It may bring a smile to your face when you realize how your actions do send a nonverbal message. The first step in improving your body language is realizing what you're doing in the first place.

BUREAUCRACY IS FRUSTRATING FOR EVERYONE

• • •

Have you ever completed one of those employee engagement surveys for your company? These are the ones where they ask for opinions on a range of topics, including corporate culture, benefits, corporate communication, and the vision for the organization coming from senior management. It enables those at the highest levels of the company to get an overall feel of the happiness and satisfaction within the organization.

There's usually good feedback, maybe a surprise or two, providing a number of opportunities for an employer to make some adjustments to improve things. However, no matter how well-run an organization is, I can pretty much guarantee that, for the vast majority companies, large and small, the same comments always appear. We wish there were fewer meetings, faster opportunities for advancement including salary growth, and issues about corporate bureaucracy.

"On a scale of one to ten, with ten being excellent, how do you feel we handle bureaucracy at our company?" Has anyone ever given anything higher than a six to this question? The reason is that when we want to hire a new staff member, order a new laptop, or just get something done today, we don't want to hear that we need three levels of approval, should have a meeting "off-line" to discuss, or wait until the new fiscal year.

Even saying the word bureaucracy can make people cringe. It's the frustrating part of any business and probably on the short list of factors of why people want to leave the corporate world and do their own thing. However, the checks and balances do keep things managed and under control. Without some of type of structured system, regulations, and procedures, I think we'd all agree that it would be pretty chaotic where we worked.

What should you do to get things done when things seem to slow to a crawl? Here are a few recommendations:

1. Don't look at it as one massive issue that crosses the entire company. That's unfixable in the short term. Focus on one issue, one area of the company, or one procedure and target that for change.
2. Complaining is okay and voicing your displeasure is acceptable, but come up with a solution, too.
3. Lead by example. No matter what your job is or what title you may have, there are responsibilities that we have that can be improved. Make your job more efficient and streamlined to get things done easier and faster.
4. I have an entry in this book about being a "Champion" for something. This is a way to be one. Be a leader, recruit others, and take on the challenge.
5. The reality is that some companies are sadly just so entrenched with anchors dragging everything to a crawl. There are people who thrive and can survive that. Don't let that be you. There is always time to find the better job and more progressive company.

CALL, EMAIL, OR TWEET YOUR OWN COMPANY

● ● ●

The recommendation to be a "customer" and test out how your company responds to communication it receives is not new advice. In fact, I remember reading about this many years ago when a magazine asked CEOs to call their companies' toll-free numbers to see how their teams handled the calls. Needless to say, there were a few surprises and some embarrassed leaders when they experienced being transferred, disconnected, or their questions left unanswered.

Today, companies need to be ready to handle not just telephone calls, but emails, comments on web pages, and tweets from customers. We also need to be able to handle feedback quickly, not twelve, fourteen, or forty-eight hours later. Customers and clients want answers to questions, more information, or responses handled immediately. The longer the wait, the more disappointed the person gets and the more likely he goes elsewhere.

It is a good idea to test this out every so often for your company or your department. You can call your own office or department and see what happens. You know the menu item on every website that says, "Contact Us"? Try that someday. Unfortunately, I think you'll be surprised. I've personally found that it is a communication mechanism that is often a red flag for slow responsiveness. Not responding or mishandling tweets can escalate into a real public relations issue.

This seems to happen often with airlines. Passengers are stuck on the tarmac for hours or some celebrity has had their luggage lost and, the next thing you know, there are Instagram photos, Facebook videos, and endless tweets. Having a social media response team is a requirement in this day and age.

Often, this responsibility falls under corporate marketing, sales, or the public relations team. One of the first things you need to know is: whose responsibility is this in your company? How is it evaluated and reviewed? Each of us needs to take the initiative to test the consumer experience by calling, emailing, and tweeting our own company. This sounds so basic, but it so often neglected.

CAREER PLANNING BY DEVELOPING PATHS

• • •

Do you have a plan in place for your career? If you don't, you're making a big mistake and could find yourself in a scary situation should your current job suddenly change. Nothing needs to be set in stone but having a few options to consider for potential next steps can only be beneficial to you.

I have recommended developing paths. There's a two-sentence overview for each, with pros and cons noted, an action plan, and a timeline. They're simple to do and you can revise them as needed.

Your first path is your current job and you "Stay the Course." There's nothing wrong with this approach. You're content, there will be annual salary increases, you like where you are, and you're not looking to be the next CEO. You're happy.

The second path takes a more "Opportunistic" approach with your current company. Your job is a good one, the company solid, you're well-liked and are a high achiever. You're making your manager aware that you want to move to the next level.

The third path is "Opportunistic-Creative," where you remain your current company but add more responsibilities linked to other departments or transfer to another department completely. Maybe it's adding some global responsibilities, being a CRM champion, adding project management work, and so forth. It's being creative to enhance your current role.

"Exploring Options with New Companies" is the one we most think of with a career path, but often after something has happened with our current job. It's my feeling that you need to keep your eyes on what's happening elsewhere. Maybe you can move your career along faster by joining another organization. Some people have this as a key career path objective.

For those with a strong stomach and hopefully some financial security, having a "Disruptive" path is an option. This is when you ask yourself, "If you could do anything, what would it be?" Maybe you start your own business? Get in on the ground floor of a start-up? Or go to school for a new specialty.

This is not just a nice-to-do exercise, I think it's critically important for all of us to have a plan for our career direction and a few paths to consider, no matter what stage of our life we are in.

CHANGE IS
INEVITABLE

● ● ●

We all can get comfortable with routines, whether it's with our job, the commute, people we work with, the direction of our company, or whatever it may be There's a feeling of stability when we know what to expect, how things should develop and when things will occur. There's nothing wrong with being comfortable and it's human nature to get accustomed and content, in knowing with what the next steps will be. However, that's not how things work in business where change is inevitable. You have to learn to process it, accept it, and to be successful, embrace it.

Look at what you were doing just five years ago. The technology you used. The key tasks on your job description. Now go back a decade and think about your job, where you worked, what your current company said about its plans in press releases and annual reports. What kind of mobile device did you use? See what I mean about change?

As an individual, change keeps us fresh, open to new ideas, and always learning new ways of doing things. Have you ever heard that person in your office say, "Well, that's the way we've always done it"? You never want to be that person. So, accept change as an inevitable part of business and be the one to lead others to adapt to it and thrive at it.

CHARISMA

● ● ●

We all run across people in our business and personal lives who have that special charisma. They're well-liked, have charm, a personality that appeals to everyone, and that gift of "presence" when they walk into a room. There are CEOs who have this quality, celebrities, politicians, and even colleagues in your department. Some people are born with it, while others develop it by listening better, growing confidence in themselves without being egotistical, and working hard to encourage and motivate others. They seem to be able to get people to follow them or be persuaded by their charismatic ways.

Always remember, just because they have this way about them, doesn't mean they are always right. Charismatic people can be wrong and they make mistakes just like the rest of us. Believe in your abilities. You can admire them, listen to them, but evaluate what they say and then follow what you believe is right.

COLLABORATION
AND TEAMWORK

● ● ●

In every industry, various departments must work together to complete projects, meet fiscal goals, and help the company be successful. Whether the departments work well together is anyone's guess. In some companies, there are silos between departments, others need referees to keep them from bickering, and a few work together, but there's a strained relationship. However, the best companies find ways to break down barriers, foster teamwork, and remain focused to support their customers, close business, and grow revenue.

In many companies, there are programs for educating employees about the roles and responsibilities of various positions. However, if your company doesn't do this or you feel like you need to know more, it would be very wise to be proactive find out.

I'd recommend you take the time to ask questions, listen, and get a better feel of the work of the following departments:

Finance: Very simply, you should have a basic grasp of how the finances work and what the profit margin goals are for your business and company. If you're weak in this subject, take a class to learn the key terminology.

Customer Care: Often, this department is in remote locations or not in the limelight and we only contact them in emergencies. They can be such a great advantage to you and relieve of a lot of work if you partner with them to support customers. Showing your interest, support, and thanking them will go a long way!

Product Development/Manufacturing: These are teams that either create a product or develop that service. You need to have a solid working knowledge of what your company can and can't do. Ignorant businesspeople from other departments really annoy these departments.

Management: Do you know by name and by function all of the leadership team of your company? You should, since you never know when you may cross paths with them and they can help you personally with one of your projects.

Sales: Don't assume you know what a sales person does. There's more time spent planning, preparing, and researching than actually asking for an order. Go work with a sales person or join one for coffee to learn more about how he or she spends a day.

Marketing: Sales and marketing have bumped heads for years. My advice? Sales people need to get over it! Learn more about what they do, and I think it will open your eyes. Make them a part of the process no what department you're in.

The most successful businesspeople spend time to learn what other departments do so they can tap into their expertise to help them do their own work better. In this competitive marketplace, companies whose employees work in silos are not successful. Collaboration and teamwork are what the best companies have mastered.

COMMON SENSE IS OFTEN THE BEST APPROACH

● ● ●

Years ago, I started a new job with a new company and I worked with some really impressive people who also had some very lofty titles. They had been in business for more years than me and many had distinguished reputations. Candidly, I was a bit intimidated when I'd listen to some of them in meetings. However, as time went on and I learned more, I began to wonder why they would make such a long ordeal out what I thought could be quick decisions. I realized that with all of their talk, they had forgotten basic common sense. Discussions, meetings, and follow-up would take place even when the answer was right in front of them.

It was a great lesson for me and one that I took to subsequent jobs. My guess is that, nine out of ten times, the answer to a problem is right in front of you and it comes down to common sense and your best instincts. Listen to your colleagues, gather information, assess the feedback, make a decision and go with your common-sense belief. You'll get things done faster, people will respond positively to the speed of decision-making and you'll be right. For the times when you're not right, apologize, regroup, and move on. It's a great formula to follow.

CONFLICTS: DON'T LET THEM FESTER— SOLVE TODAY

● ● ●

This is good advice to follow when handling disagreements in both our personal lives and in business settings. Conflicts and disagreements will happen; they're simply part of life. It's how you handle them and solve them that is the key. Having said that, conflicts in business shouldn't be avoided either. In Patrick Lencioni's million-copy bestseller, *The Five Dysfunctions of a Team*, one of his key points is that conflict is good and healthy for an organization. It ties in with being open, honest, and addressing issues that can be negatively impacting our business. I agree completely, and it's on my list of some of the best advice I've ever followed. It also aligns with the statement, "This is business, and it's not personal."

Where I draw the line, though, is when conflicts become petty and annoying. I think you know what I mean. A coworker takes issue with someone else's negative comment, a person embarrasses a colleague when he's late for a meeting, or you take offense to being ridiculed about the proposal you've made. It moves from a conflict to childish tactics of not speaking to one another, people gossiping about the people involved, and it goes on for a few days. Sadly, these situations aren't uncommon, and they are totally unprofessional. All parties come away looking inadequate, amateurish, and, candidly, really juvenile.

Honesty, candor, and being direct are effective in making the business run better. However, when it progresses to the next stage, be aware of those situations. Hopefully, there's an effective manager who nips those things in the bud, but you need to recognize it too. Petty conflict hurts the business and, just as important, can make you look weak too. The last thing you want is to make a trip to human resources for conflict resolution. So, don't let them fester. Meet with the person, hash it out, solve it, and move on. Today.

CONSIDER HIRING
A COACH

• • •

When I first got into business, there really wasn't the opportunity to work with a coach to help me improve my skills. There were training programs and things I learned from my manager, but professional "coaches" didn't really exist. There were those who worked with the senior executives of a company as consultants and there were some executive coaches, but for the rest of the lower-level employees, it was difficult to find someone to help them.

Today, there is certainly no shortage of coaches. There are coaches who specialize in everything from career planning to leadership development and from life challenges to business skills. Over the past few years, there has been a proliferation of coaches and it is becoming much more common for people at all levels in a company to seek them out.

You can do 360 peer reviews, have assessments done, and get detailed performance appraisals from your manager, but it's so different when you hire a coach. There's no link to your company, you do it confidentially, and the honesty with no "baggage" can make the process very rewarding. You can open up and express yourself without any fear of a colleague, manager, or peer finding out. The focus is on finding ways for you to improve, be a stronger leader, enjoy work more, or find a new career opportunity.

With there being so many coaches available to choose from and with so many specialties, you need to do your research just as you would do before hiring anyone. Word of mouth is always a good approach and you can also look online for those based locally. LinkedIn has a program called ProFinder (*https://www. linkedin.com/profinder*) where you can put in a confidential request for a specialized coach. You'll get five proposals, a free consultation, evaluate, and then you can decide if there's one you want to work with going forward.

If you think that after five, ten, or even twenty years you don't need continue with training, you're wrong. The changes in the marketplace, technology, and leadership techniques should make us seek individualized coaching throughout our careers. I think the most effective businesspeople do this without hesitation. Consider consulting a coach every once in a while, as an investment in yourself.

CORPORATE CULTURE IS SO IMPORTANT

• • •

You can have a job with a great title and a salary that makes you feel really good every time it's payday, but if it's a struggle to go work each Monday, then that's a big problem. The culture of your employer is as important as the compensation you receive, your job responsibility, and any perks that may be tied to it.

My definition of corporate culture may be a bit simplistic, but I say culture ties right in with whether your company is a place you enjoy working at each day. It's a place where your peers are not just smart but fun to be with, senior management listens and knows how to lead, and there's a path (vision) of where you're all headed.

Based on my unscientific findings it doesn't take an advanced degree to conclude that it's more fun to work with people you like. It's also clear that some leaders and companies are a lot better at encouraging, motivating, and empowering. I believe that, in most cases, the companies noted for having a good culture are the ones with colleagues who are nice, authentic, and outgoing. Weak companies are linked to adjectives that include the words selfish, uncaring, and stressful.

Impacting culture is the direction and the modeling of the behavior that should start at the very top of the organization.

Great leaders are ones who recognize that culture is an essential factor in the success of a company. Achieving revenue and profitability targets does help a lot, but it's not everything. People need to know they are a part of the overall mission. When they feel they have some ownership, there are a lot more smiles around an office than with those companies where colleagues are unheard and considered to be "head count."

Over the course of my career, I've worked with three companies for an extended period of time. Each have had exceptional success, different corporate personalities and unique cultures. For me, during my times there, one was more laid back and maybe let some opportunities pass them by. Another was very intense and had great financial results, but I sure wouldn't say it was fun to be at every day. The third one experienced amazing growth through the years and the team of leaders were visible, collaborative, and even stressed making it "The Place to Be." That slogan sends a meaningful message, doesn't it? It was conveyed from the senior levels and spread across the entire organization to create a very special environment.

A good corporate culture doesn't happen by accident. It happens when great leaders are in place and they hire those who can see a similar vision. They value the goal of success and happiness as a team. They know culture is a critical ingredient to the health of the company.

When those factors aren't in place, and you feel unhappy or unfulfilled and the culture is unpleasant, then you need to look for something more fulfilling and rewarding.

COUNT TO TEN
AND TAKE A
BREATH BEFORE
RESPONDING

● ● ●

We've all made that telephone call to a customer service department and have been transferred a few times, tried unsuccessfully to navigate the confusing menu options, or after being on hold for twenty minutes, get disconnected. We've all had the driver behind us honk his horn really loudly when we were a second too slow from moving after the light turned green. We've all experienced being in a long and slow check-out line when someone cuts in front of everybody.

How do you handle those situations? It's amazing how some people can go from being calm and respectful to suddenly having their voice go up a few decibels and their eyes starting to glare like an angry bear. There are others, though, who just have the great ability to let things roll off their back, they remain calm, and don't let things like that bother them to the same degree.

Counting to ten really means you stop and think about your response before you actually do anything. This is especially important when you're in stressful or confrontational situations. I think we've all seen that person at the airport check-in who has some issue with his seat or concern about missing a connection. People who would normally be so professional are just the opposite. In the end, their lack of control is not helping them at all and, in fact, their anger is making things worse.

Taking a breath, remaining calm, and being more careful with our response takes some work and concentration. Effective and respected business professionals understand the importance of managing their emotions, how to give feedback in pressured situations, and also when to seek advice if things become more of an anger management problem. The phrase "counting to ten," focuses specifically on being composed and not letting your emotions take over. Whatever technique you use, it's important to follow it.

CREATIVITY

• • •

"Okay, everybody, let's be creative." I actually once heard a manager say that to a group of us in a windowless meeting room at the end of a long week. That's like saying to a comedian, "Hey, be funny." It's just not that easy.

Creativity comes naturally to some people. They've got ideas they're always ready to tell people about, they are able to express them easily, and do so with such enthusiasm. They can be from any department, but I always found that the marketing teams and the business development groups were always ready to toss out new concepts and imaginative new ideas. They were never shy about unleashing their creativity.

For the rest of us, we need to be in the right mood, or the right setting and, most importantly, feel comfortable opening up. I actually think that last point is the most important. Sometimes we feel a bit embarrassed or not confident about expressing some creative new idea out of fear that others may think it's not worthy or it's silly. That's an inhibition that we all need to work on overcoming.

Creativity is what drives innovation, new and better ways of doing things, and opens up our vision to what can be done. Creativity can be closely linked to inspiration too. Think of companies like Apple, Amazon, Netflix, and Salesforce which always seem to appear on lists of innovative organizations. However, creativity can and should flourish no matter what the size of company you work for or what your title is. This is something that is in your power to do. Don't sit back hesitating. Participate, let your mind imagine new ideas and concepts, and enable the creativity that you have to come to the surface.

CREDIBILITY

• • •

Credibility is on my short list of qualities that I consider essential for every employee. If you are credible, you are trustworthy and believable. There is also the critical factor that people see you as someone with expertise and what you say carries weight. It doesn't get more straightforward than that and its importance in business cannot be understated.

How do you want your manager to think of you? If your job connects with those outside of the company, such as in sales and marketing, isn't credibility essential with your customers and accounts? If you manage people, being trusted, believable, and respected for your expertise is essential. With your peers and coworkers, you always want to be respected as the colleague who can be relied on, is honest, and knows your specialty to the best of your ability.

Credibility is such a valuable quality and must be always kept to the highest standards. I consider it one of the cornerstones to being a successful and respected business professional. Losing or having your credibility damaged can take a long time, if ever, to regain. Protect it, value it, and always remain a trusted and believable person whose expertise in your work is top priority.

CUSTOMER RELATIONSHIP MANAGEMENT SOFTWARE (CRM)

● ● ●

You may assume that customer relationship management software is just for sales people. They may be the primary users and suppliers of information for it, but the data supplied is critical for every department in a company. The ability to collaborate enables companies to work more efficiently than ever, and I think CRMs are now one of the most important tools in a company.

Many of you may remember the days before CRM. Depending on your employer, sales people kept their account information in a variety of formats. They stored it on spreadsheets, in unsophisticated databases, and even on some off-the-shelf rogue account-tracking software that could be bought at office supply stores. No one had easy access to critical account and market information.

Today, all of our businesses are much more competitive, and we can no longer afford not to share account data with others in our companies. Candidly, not doing so puts you at a real disadvantage. Thankfully, we have much better tools than what we had just a few years ago. CRMs have become so much more user-friendly and have become an integral part of most organizations computer systems.

They integrate well with technology tools ranging from customer care support to lead generation software. Some even work with LinkedIn to enable networking with professionals globally. The value of the detailed account information in our CRMs assists all departments involved with the sales process to greatly improve their efficiency.

I think CRM implementation and usage is now one of the most critical tools and responsibilities within an organization. The following five factors are the key benefits:

- Leads, Opportunities, Close Rates: All of this information is now in one location, rather than in rogue databases and spreadsheets. You can create the fields to track this information and so much more, enabling you to get a real feel of the sales pipeline.

- Forecasting: This cuts down on the time to prepare a forecast, since everyone's numbers are there and weighted by potential close percentages. Accuracy of projections improve dramatically and it can be done rapidly.

- Market Feedback: I think the level and quality of feedback from sales professionals is an important performance measurement. The CRM enables all staff to input data in a consistent way and enables managers, along with other critical departments to retrieve it easily.

- Analysis by Channel: The reviews of accounts by channel, resources spent, revenue achieved, and cost-to-sales ratios calculated can be measured efficiently.

- Team Work and Engagement: Departments working together to focus on plans to provide solutions to customers is what we all are trying to accomplish. The CRM encourages and reinforces that important objective.

Using CRMs does mean that our companies must reinforce and require its use. Management must model the way and be visible adding their input and feedback. Regardless of your position, you must use the CRM for performance management analyses because it is indispensable.

DELEGATE

● ● ●

Delegating or, more specifically, the inability to delegate is a bigger issue than you may suspect. It not only has a negative impact on the person who fails to give up responsibilities, but also on the person who should be taking on those tasks and developing in his role.

There are a number of reasons why we fail to delegate. Sometimes it's because we know we can get the task done in short order and, if we let someone else do it, it could take much longer. We rationalize this by saying, "Oh, let me just do it, get it done, and get out of the way."

Tied to that is that we're too stubborn or lazy to want to train someone to take over a task we're currently handling. It's true that when you delegate, you have to take the time and effort to train someone to do a particular task.

There are a number of responsibilities that we have that we ignorantly and egotistically think that we can just do better than anyone else. It may be something we've "owned," for years even though it is no longer part of our job description, but we just don't want to give it up.

To be an effective leader, to grow your team, and to build a stronger organization you must also learn to delegate tasks so you, too, can grow and be the leader you're supposed to be. Make the time to train people, don't micromanage the process, and if you do this properly, your staff will become more motivated and your chances for even greater success improve dramatically.

Make a list of three things you can delegate over the next sixty days. It's a great exercise that will pay you in dividends.

DELIVER ON YOUR PROMISE

• • •

There are a number of characteristics and qualities that I call critical "basics" of being a business professional. Honoring the commitments you give to your business connections, your customers and your colleagues is one that I believe is so important. It goes to the core of your credibility and reputation. It may seem straightforward, but if you say you're going to do something by a certain date, then quite simply, you have to deliver on that promise.

The pressure to complete all aspects of our jobs is taken for granted in today's competitive business environment. We will always face some type of deadline, forecast that we must hit, and expectations that, at times, may seem a bit more than a stretch. That's when we can run the risk of cutting a few corners, making a few promises that may be tough to honor, or giving a commitment that will require some good breaks along the way. It's one thing to lay out an aggressive timeline or complicated service plan that will require 100 percent effort to complete. However, there are some real ethical issues when you commit to something that you know has high risk for completion.

A number of years ago, I was working with an account to which I had been trying to sell to for a long time. If the program was approved, it was going to be a really large order and make my year. Finally, the day came and the buyer called with a purchase order, but it included some additional customization that was required. I went to our development teams who gave me an updated timeline and delivery schedule based on these changes. There was very little wiggle room, but I didn't tell the buyer that and just said we could commit to the required delivery dates.

I got the order, it was a really big one, and for the new few weeks, instead of being happy, I was a nervous wreck. I got lucky and the order arrived in plenty of time, but I should have been upfront with the buyer about the tight schedule. If it had been late, my credibility would have been ruined forever, but more importantly, it would have put my buyer in a bad situation too.

As businesspeople, our reputation and our credibility are the backbone of how we are perceived by our contacts and peers. If we fail to deliver on our commitments and promises, this cuts right to the core of our personal integrity. We can never afford to lose that and must ensure that our standards stay at the highest levels.

DEVELOPING SELF-CONFIDENCE AND BELIEVING IN YOURSELF

● ● ●

This seems so straight-forward and simple, doesn't it? Be self-confident and believe in yourself! We watch seminars from outgoing and charismatic presenters telling us how to be better, we read books about how to be the person we always wanted to be, or we watch webinars or read articles about the subject too.

In fact, I think developing self-confidence is probably one of the hardest skills to learn and maintain over a period of time. You can be the smartest person at the university or the one who barely passes, the most brilliant employee at the company or the one who barely meets minimum requirements, and you could the life of the party or the more reserved conservative type. I don't care if you're a CEO or a new entry-level sales-person, the reality is, self-confidence is a challenge for all of us at times. The difference, though, is the experience some people have in knowing the techniques to overcome the blue attitude that hits us all from time to time.

Very often, you'll find that having an upbeat personality and being confident go hand-in-hand or feed off each other. Surrounding yourself with positive people versus negative people can often help you feel better about yourself. The same holds true for the managers we work for and colleagues who are our peers. Those who are supportive, give good quality feedback to you, and recognize or reward your efforts can motivate you and build your confidence. You can't change jobs in a flash or the people around you, but be very wary of the impact of a poor leader and negative people as they can drain your self-esteem and enjoyment of your work.

However, developing your confidence is more than just improving your surroundings; it's how you assess yourself and how you feel deep down about your work, your personal life, and "you," in general. Frankly, some people just have the ability to feel good about themselves the majority of the time. In fact, we all know a few who sometimes go overboard with their confidence and actually need a lesson in how to keep their ego in check.

For me, I've found that every so often I try to take a step back and evaluate how I think things are progressing with my work, my career, and my personal life. I do this in an informal way and don't try overanalyze things and I review things in small pieces. I used to be very hard on myself in the middle stages of my career and then, as I studied confidence more, I realized that it's okay to not be perfect. Maybe I could have done things differently but I'm happy and I feel good about myself.

Pick a time for yourself someday and do an informal self-evaluation. Maybe it's a quiet hour on your weekend or while you're on a peaceful walk some evening. When you do this, I guarantee you'll probably be overly-critical of yourself. However, I think we all should be prouder of our accomplishments, big and small. I also think if your self-esteem has been in the dumps for too long then the smart move is to seek some additional professional guidance. And there's nothing wrong with doing that.

In business, you have to be able to accept the highs and lows of your work. And being self-confident is an important skill. Our contacts respond to people who are upbeat, positive, and self-assured. Yes, building your self-confidence is not easy to master, but it's a critical ingredient for your business success and personal growth.

DIFFERENCE
BETWEEN
ACQUAINTANCES,
CONNECTIONS
& COLLEAGUES,
FRIENDS, & FAMILY

• • •

This is a subject I learned more about as I progressed in my career. You might find this to be a bit of a depressing entry, but bear with me.

It's something in my work as a career and executive coach I talk about with my clients. There's the tough reality that we need to recognize that our list of truly close contacts, people we can really count on, is a lot smaller than we realize. Clients work with me as they're looking for a new job or to change careers and they say they're going to reach out to hundreds of their close connections. It can be upsetting when the hundreds turn out to be just dozens.

Over the course of our careers, we meet hundreds of people. With some positions in sales and marketing, we may meet thousands. This is especially true if we have changed jobs many times. There are those in our company, attendees at meetings, and introductions from those we meet along the way. We know their names, we say hi in the cafeteria, and may even exchange cards at a conference. These are acquaintances.

Colleagues and connections from the various departments we've worked in or met regularly from other companies can add up to a good number of people. We get to know more about them, their families, and maybe we've had lunches with them too. Think back to those from your first job. How many with whom are you still in close contact? Many of these are the connections you have on LinkedIn, hundreds of former co-workers, or contacts you had with other companies.

It's like that graphic used to show the sales and marketing funnel. It starts really wide at the top and then, as it funnels, it gets smaller and smaller.

We can all have a good conversation with an acquaintance and talk about business or market trends. We have a drink with a former colleague and tell stories about the good old days. However, when you need to get something accomplished, a favor, a lead, an introduction to a new job opportunity, you must also be realistic with expectations as to how many can and will really assist you.

Cultivate and stay close to your real friends. Reflect on this entry as the message is so true.

DO IT NOW—DON'T PROCRASTINATE

● ● ●

Have you ever watched a magician with a deck of cards and he moves them around on a table from left to right and right to left, nothing gets picked up, and then you're supposed to pick one out the group?

It's a similar feeling when we have ten projects we know we have to do, fifty unopened emails, as well as the list of objectives from our manager. We look at everything, we reread notes, and maybe open a few of those emails, but then we get frustrated because we haven't done anything. We are like the magician moving things around.

We all fall into the trap of procrastinating every so often for a variety of reasons. We may be overwhelmed with work and not know where to start. The list of things we have to do isn't fun and, frankly, we don't want to do any of them. Or we don't have a good action plan in place, with deadlines to get things done.

There are many problems that can arise when we procrastinate. We're all aware that it can make us look bad, can increase our stress levels, and the work isn't going to miraculously go away. However, we have all fallen into this trap and we all know a coworker who has problems with this. It can really impact business and career opportunities. You don't want to be known as a person who stalls or, worse yet, doesn't get things done.

This is why I focus so much on organizational skills, planning, and preparation. The time you take to map out your work will enable you focus clearly on what needs to be accomplished. I also recommend assigning a timeframe with deadlines for anything important. It does make a difference when you lay out a schedule. It reinforces the objective to do it now.

DON'T ARGUE WITH
YOUR BOSS

● ● ●

There are a number of lessons that can be learned from this entry about not arguing with your boss. However, before I go on, let's clarify the seemingly obvious assumption that every manager and direct report relationship is different.

Some of you will have an open and honest situation, while others of you may have one that always seems to be strained. A one-size-fits-all recommendation does not apply here. Given the consequences of a poor decision on your part concerning an action with your boss, getting a second opinion is always warranted before proceeding. My thoughts here are general in nature and you need see how best they can be applied to your own working relationship with your boss.

The simple advice is that arguing with your manager is not worth it. Clearly, sticking up for your beliefs and decision-making is important. In fact, I've always liked it when someone I managed called me out diplomatically to say he thought I was wrong. He knew the situation better than me and stuck to his reasoning to show where I had erred. There may have been some back-and-forth discussion, but that's healthy, and the sign of a strong working relationship.

However, when a discussion escalates to the next level, it's a losing proposition. Every so often, we'll hear about a colleague confronting his manager in an office. Hopefully, that's done privately and no one else is aware of their discussion. However, even if the conversation is private, if it is confrontational, it will take a long time, if ever, to repair the damage. If done publicly and voices get loud, let's say in a group meeting, then my guess is that the employee will be moving to find a new opportunity sooner rather than ever.

We all have moments with our managers when we throw up our arms, wondering what they're thinking. We even go back and forth, maybe with more direct and stern communication. However, if you report to someone with whom you're arguing frequently, rather than occasionally, that's not a good situation. You're not working for the right person and maybe you need to take steps to find a better manager or different employer.

DON'T BE AFRAID TO SAY "NO"

• • •

Throughout our lives, we often experience pressure to participate, show support, and say "yes," that we can join a meeting, be in that task force, or help support some local cause. We all want to help and be there to lend a hand or be that positive voice for our manager or a co-worker. However, how many times have you said to yourself, "Why did I say yes and agree to do this?"

We say, "Yes," and then we find ourselves struggling to fulfill our commitment. Our other work suffers and we also end up not doing a great job with the task we agreed to help out on. We need to learn to respect our time, realize we can't do everything, and not feel guilty when we say, "No." It comes down to being honest with yourself and realistic to the person asking you. It's much better to be upfront right from the beginning, rather than backtracking later on. So, don't be afraid to say, "No."

DON'T BE AFRAID TO
SAY "I DON'T KNOW"

● ● ●

A situation that I'm about to describe is very common and predictable. You're sitting in a meeting or you're watching a presentation and a statement is made that is a bit confusing or an uncommon acronym is used. The speaker continues or maybe even asks, "Does everyone understand?" There's an awkward silence, some people turn to look back to their notes like they're hiding, and maybe one or two people tentatively start to raise their hands but stop. Finally, a brave soul says, "I don't understand" or, "I don't know." I guarantee, if you then look around the room, at least one third of the attendees are nodding they don't know either.

We behave like this because we're afraid of appearing ignorant or feeling like we're the only one who doesn't know the answer. It's actually human nature. I was like that for years and then, at breaks or at the end of meetings, I'd research the notes that I didn't comprehend. It's pretty silly, isn't it? It's actually a sign of confidence and good leadership if you do raise your hand, ask that question, and not be shy. My guess is, most of the time, you're not alone and others will appreciate your willingness to speak up, ask for clarification, and that you're not afraid to say that you don't know.

DON'T BE THE "YES" PERSON

● ● ●

There are a number of ways you could interpret this entry. You could see it as being the person who always agrees to help with a project, no matter how busy you are. You're the one who's afraid to say, "No," for fear of offending someone so you just say, "Yes." Or maybe you commit to something when you really shouldn't have (See the entry for Deliver on Your Promise).

The one I want to specifically focus on is the person who agrees to everything said by her manager, someone in power, or a colleague who may be proposing something. This individual can be found in every company and the individual's act is so obvious that, in the long run, it ends up alienating the employee from the rest of the group.

They are the colleagues who, in an effort to be supportive, are people-pleasers and come across as phony. They blindly believe that, by acting favorably, it will be advantageous to them in the long run. Sadly, we all know they say and do things solely to reap the benefit from doing so. It's really such a weakness to try seek approval in this way and it tarnishes credibility. Someone who kisses up doesn't have a good reputation among the other employees.

We need to be real, authentic, and never have our integrity tarnished. The "Yes" person is someone who you just can't trust and not someone with whom you want to work. It's definitely a characteristic that you don't want associated with your reputation.

DON'T BURN
BRIDGES

● ● ●

Many years ago, I worked for a manager who, candidly, was pretty mediocre. He was a real micromanager, not a great leader, and, to make matters worse, he would take credit for work that his staff had actually done. When I was ready to leave that company, my relationship with him was frustrating and I knew it was time to move on to a new, more enjoyable position. In my last meeting with him, I was so tempted to be honest about how poor of a manager I thought he was. I smiled as I thought of all of the great one-liners I was going to say to him and finally have my day to put him in his place.

The night before that meeting, I remembered reading about the phrase: Don't Burn Bridges. That phrase comes from the idea that, if you use a bridge to cross a river and then burn it, you can't get back over the river if you need to do so in the future. In business, it would translate to breaking a relationship and making it impossible to ever work or communicate with that person or that company ever again. So, at that meeting with my manager, I took a deep breath and expressed my thanks for my time spent at that company and the experience of working with him. We parted professionally, cordially, and he had no idea that I was so thrilled to be moving on.

A few years later, I went on an account visit with one of the salespeople from my team to make a presentation to a group of executives from a company outside of our traditional sales channels. I walked into the meeting room and my stomach tightened when I saw the manager for whom I had worked. He had left his position shortly after me and changed careers to work this at this new up-and-coming startup. I held my breath and then he smiled, introducing me to the other attendees, saying we were close colleagues working at "x" company and I was someone who came with great credentials. You think I was relieved?

By the way, we ended up working on a number of projects together over the next few years. I realized that I was probably a part of the problem at my old job and I ended up telling him this story. We laughed as he admitted his management skills were a bit lacking back then too. If I had burned that bridge, it would have cost me in many ways.

DON'T BURN BRIDGES, TAKE THE HIGH ROAD

● ● ●

There's another great phrase called, "Taking the High Road." It's doing something that maybe deep down you don't want to but you're being a class act, showing restraint, and doing the right thing, even if it's not easy. I was glad I had followed that advice with regards to my prior manager.

Today, we are all connected much closer than ever before. I think one of the best illustrations is when we're on LinkedIn and we see how closely we are connected with people we may assume are strangers. Burning a bridge and the impact that can have is evident with information that can spread quickly, whether someone is researching you for a new job, is a potential customer, or a client getting background details about you.

This doesn't mean that when you've been wronged, mistreated, or managed inappropriately you shouldn't stick up for your rights. In fact, it is so important that in cases like that you do make the appropriate staff aware and handle it professionally.

However, giving someone "a piece of your mind" or "venting" during that exit interview or arguing during a business meeting that hasn't gone well, may feel good for thirty seconds, but the long-term impact over time may be irreparable. So, keep that in mind, should you ever encounter a situation like that and, remember, take the high road and don't burn bridges.

DON'T FORGET THE SMALL DETAILS

● ● ●

No matter what our jobs are, the most important elements are clearly the top three, four, or five objectives that we'll find on our job descriptions. My first sales manager narrowed it down to just two. He said to me early in my career, "Dean, I'm going to make this simple for you. Your job is be focused on hitting and then exceeding your sales budget, while at the same time making sure you spend less than your expense budget." He was very clear in his approach, since he didn't want us to ever forget the real objective of our jobs and get derailed with the dozens of items we may have had on our "to-do" list.

I believe in that philosophy of a laser-focused approach. We were hired to perform a small list of critical objectives. It doesn't matter what our jobs or titles may be, but there are those key tasks that drive the success or disappointment of our work.

Why, then, am I including this entry about not forgetting the small details? The key objectives are what drive your business and your job, but it is the small details that are missed that can negatively impact your overall plan. You don't let the minor matters slow you down and like a bestselling book says, Don't Sweat the Small Stuff. However, someone needs to make sure the little things are completed and checked off. These are ideal assignments for someone new to your team or a colleague not yet at your level to gain experience. It's the perfect way to delegate while you focus on the big items; let someone else keep an eye on the small details.

DON'T HOLD BACK
TELLING BAD NEWS

● ● ●

D o you know what's worse than having to tell people bad news? It's waiting and telling them later. It sounds like I'm kidding, but I'm being absolutely serious.

None of us ever want to pass along bad news because we know the reaction is not going to be good. People might get upset or angry if we're the ones who have to deliver that message.

It's human nature for any of us to worry, lose sleep, hem and haw, and then finally break the news to our manager, a customer, or coworker.

However, if you were to ask senior managers about bad news, I can guarantee they want to know as soon as possible. Sure, they may be unhappy, but the sooner they get word that there's a problem or an issue, the faster steps can be taken to correct the situation. Managers get really mad when we wait to tell them because, by that time, the problem has gotten worse.

Relaying tough news to a colleague or direct report is really painful too. You might have to address a poor performance issue or, even worse, have to let someone go. I've seen managers get physically ill preparing for these situations. They'll practice a speech, get incredibly stressed out, and it impacts all of their other work.

The fact is people are smarter and more aware of the situation than we suspect. People know, they sense it, and can recognize the signals. It's become torture for them to wait.

How often have you heard people say, "I'm just glad it's over? I've been so upset and nervous waiting"?

When we delay the inevitable, whether telling our manager about some business problem or a coworker about a serious matter, you make it far worse for everyone and yourself. Take a deep breath, focus your message, and deliver it today.

DON'T REST ON YOUR LAURELS

• • •

There's nothing more enjoyable than getting outstanding feedback for a marketing plan you've developed, a sale you've closed, or a project strategy implemented to perfection. We all need a salary to survive, but personal satisfaction of hearing from your manager, colleagues, or the marketplace that your work is well done is a great feeling.

I believe we actually need to celebrate and take more stock of the good work that we all do. Sometimes, in the pressure to perform, we don't stop to pass along compliments and reward our colleagues. Stepping back to acknowledge our efforts is a critically important motivator and helps energize us to move on.

Now, having said that, here's the toss of cold water. In life, and especially in business, you can't rest on your laurels. That means that you can't just stop and be satisfied with your current success, you have to continue on. A more direct way to say this is that you're only as good as your last achievement.

So, celebrate your work and accept the accolades. You can even pat yourself on the back, but don't think that you're done and everything will now come easily for you. Unfortunately, it won't. Your manager, your customers, or other colleagues will be looking for you to produce at the same top level again. Strive to do it even better the next time, set the bar higher, and never rest on your laurels.

DON'T SHOW OFF
OR GLOAT

● ● ●

There's always someone gloating or showing off in every office. It doesn't matter if it's a Fortune 500 company or a small startup. There's always that one person who likes to show off and some other colleague who is always gloating about something he did. What do you think of people like that?

There have been many articles written by psychologists about why some people like to display themselves in a certain way to gain attention. The show-offs may talk about some new possession such as a new car, designer clothing, or a new piece of jewelry. The gloater walks around telling people about a promotion, a big deal he closed, or the meeting he was in with the company CEO.

Are they seeking acceptance? Do they feel neglected by the rest of us? Is their ego so fragile that they need to show off or gloat? I don't know, but it might be a little of each of those things. However, once you have this type of reputation, it's tough to shake it off and it can set you back in your career.

Let your results or actions speak for themselves. There's no need to show off to others or let people hear about your accomplishments from you. People can figure out what you've accomplished. By taking a more modest approach, you'll be much better liked and respected.

DON'T TAKE ALL OF THE CREDIT— SHARE THE WINS

● ● ●

We've probably all come across that person who always seems to want to take the credit for some accomplishment, successful project, or results from a winning deal. When the company president extends congratulations, they are the ones who raise their hands or stand up, as if they're taking a bow. Do you also notice that everyone else cringes or makes a face of annoyance? There's a lesson in that.

People who consistently take the credit for work done with others are "outed" pretty quickly. If you take credit for yourself, chances are you'll be blocked from other opportunities and become isolated from your colleagues.

Collaboration, teamwork, and a unified effort are important ingredients for a successful organization. It has a major impact on a positive corporate culture too. We respect those people who don't take all of the credit and share the wins.

Here are some real-world examples. An actress wins an Oscar but recognizes the writers, director, other actors, and support staff for making it possible. The athlete holds the trophy but says there's no way it could have happened without his exceptional teammates. The writer calls out the editor, production person, and marketer who improved the content and helped garner visibility for the book. I think we all respect those people more than the ones who just say, "Me," or, "I."

If you have worked hard and are good at what you do, you don't need to take all the credit. People already know that you're a valuable and respected coworker. Make sure you share the wins and let everyone celebrate successes as a team. Business is a lot more fun that way.

EMAIL ADDRESS FOR YOUR WORK AND ONE FOR YOUR PERSONAL LIFE: KEEP THE MAIL SEPARATE

● ● ●

This may seem like an obvious recommendation, but I know I'm not the only one who used to have just one email address for business and personal correspondence. Since the inception of email, I had just used my business address to get everything from work-related messages, to invoices from the electric company, and notes from my sister. I had it all in one spot and, in many respects, it was convenient. However, as time went on, it made everything a blur, with work creeping more and more into my personal life and vice versa. I found myself reading an email from my doctor's office and then the next email was a request for sales forecast from a financial manager in my company.

In the past, people remained with employers for longer periods of time and having one email address may have been the norm. However, now, with peopling changing jobs more often, it makes sense to have a business and a personal email account.

If you are ever going to be successful in managing the balance between work and your personal life, an important step is to ensure that you keep your emails in two distinct worlds. Also, of critical importance is that you keep your personal information off of your company's backup files. That information never really gets deleted. So, take full advantage of your personal email address and keep the business emails where they belong—at work.

EMAIL MANAGEMENT IS IMPORTANT, UP TO A POINT

● ● ●

How many articles have been written about this subject? Online courses? Training classes? All of those and more to help you manage how you handle emails. Yet have any of us solved it? Do we even need to worry about it in the first place?

Everyone has a different philosophy about how to handle emails. I'm not going to offer you any new provocative thinking or miracle solutions for handling business emails that seems to grow like weeds in our inboxes.

We've all seen people obsessed with keeping on top of every email that comes in, rather than focusing on accomplishing the tasks that are really driving the business. Then there are those who have hundreds or even thousands of unopened emails. Both types make me cringe.

What to do? Again, I'm not going to be able to change your current habits, but you need to have a strategy. Do you open your email throughout the day or do you have set times to respond, delete, or forward? Whatever works for you is fine by me.

However, in my view, you have to be able to spot and respond quickly to critical email. If business is ever lost or delayed or your manager's email is buried in with dozens of unsolicited messages, then you need to take another email management class to come up with a new plan. Our email should never control us or, due to poor handling, negatively impact business, but you need to take the necessary steps to ensure that never happens. Having an email strategy is important.

EMAIL—
SUBJECT LINE
HEADERS

● ● ●

This seems like a simple task to manage correctly, but you'd be surprised at how many people don't think about subject lines. The right subject line can be the difference between the recipient opening the email or deleting it. It can be an effective way to garner attention if you're trying to get an appointment or market your product or service.

You should keep them short, focused, and go right to the point. The emphasis on "key" words is a smart model to follow. Just as important are things you shouldn't do. Some people mistake the subject line for a text message and ramble on for a full sentence. Others leave it blank, assuming since their names are visible, you'll obviously open the email. Wrong.

Here are three that annoy me. "FYI"—Well, that says nothing and basically tells me I can read it later or never. If you put "Urgent" in the header it sure better be urgent, or any future emails from you will lose credibility. The other one is "HELP." We've all gotten one of those and we fear that someone really does need help, so we do quickly open it. For me, 100 percent of the time, the email wasn't a real need for help, but a request for more details with the sender wanting to know the name of a restaurant, or some other simple appeal.

On the priority scale of business skills to master, this one isn't near the top, but it is worth your time thinking about improving how you're handling it now and doing it more effectively.

EMOTIONAL INTELLIGENCE— EQ IS A VALUABLE SKILL

● ● ●

EQ stands for "emotional quotient" and EI for "emotional intelligence." I've found them to be used interchangeably, so for this entry, I'm to stick with the more often used EQ. I like this simple and straightforward definition from Harvard professor Howard Gardner: "Your EQ is the level of your ability to understand other people, what motivates them, and how to work cooperatively with them." This one sentence is so clear and is applicable regardless of your position or whether you manage any people.

There are some who question whether EQ can be proven and if it is truly something that has a place in business and our personal lives. I don't want to provide a scientific analysis of the validity or not of EQ. However, from my point of view, I think studying more and enhancing your emotional intelligence skills are among the most important things you need to do throughout the course of your career.

You should start by reading Daniel Goleman's bestselling book, *Emotional Intelligence,* published in 1995 and updated in 2005. I would also recommend reading *Emotional Intelligence 2.0* by Travis Bradberry that includes a test you can take to assess your EQ level. There are so many articles, classes, and online courses available and I'd encourage you take advantage of as many as you can.

Goleman frames EQ around five elements: Self Awareness, Self-Regulation, Motivation, Empathy, and Social Skills. Much of this book can be linked to these five components. They all tie into being aware, caring for others, working hard to understand others' needs and desires, and truly listening to what others are saying.

If there's one take-away I want you to have after you finish reading this book, it is the necessity to learn more about EQ, understand its importance, and value the impact it can have on your business success and personal fulfillment.

ENCOURAGE AND MOTIVATE OTHERS

● ● ●

For most of my career, I have been fortunate enough to work at companies where the corporate culture was positive, engaged, and there was a genuine, upbeat environment. During the times when that wasn't evident, it was actually a great learning experience for me, as I witnessed the impact of a negative and unsupportive atmosphere. It was clear that those "leaders" didn't understand the importance of encouragement and motivation. Without it, they had an unhappy and underperforming organization.

That really should be a very easy lesson to understand and implement. However, throughout my career, I have always been alarmed at how many people tell me that they don't feel rewarded or supported in their current companies. Motivating, encouraging, inspiring, and coaching are the basic cornerstones of being a successful leader.

However, you don't need to be a manager or executive to have these skills. Some of the best colleagues to work with are peers who reach out to support, applaud, and cheer on their coworkers. You can do that no matter what level within an organization you are or what title you have.

Encouraging and motivating fosters a strong culture, a positive work environment, and, more often than not, a company with a successful track record.

ENTHUSIASM IS CONTAGIOUS

● ● ●

It's fun to work with people who are excited, energetic, and enthusiastic about what they do. Now, before you groan, I don't mean the people who are constantly cheerleading over some of the most basic things. I mean those "Champions," "Leaders," or "Charismatic" colleagues who truly enjoy their work, believe in the objectives and mission they follow, and are realistically enthusiastic.

I hope you get chance to work with a team of people that's really in sync. That's when ideas flow easily, discussions are open and honest, and real progress is made every time you meet. The other times may be if you're a marketer, in business development, or in sales and have a product or service offering that is innovative and catches the marketplace by storm. Or maybe you're a part of a senior management team or in finance and the ideas you've implemented are showing a return on investment that is surpassing expectations. Those are situations that make all of the hard work worthwhile and generates enthusiasm that is contagious.

That doesn't happen all of the time, but the opportunities for it to occur are possible. Seek out colleagues, departments, or companies to work for where this is likely to happen more often. There's nothing more fun in business than when everyone is on board a winning and enthusiastic team.

ETHICAL BEHAVIOR

• • •

It's unfortunate that, in all walks of life and every profession, there is a small percentage of people who stray from proper ethical behavior. These people may have been well-regarded employees for years or a recent graduate of a first-rate university. For whatever reason, people who we would never suspect do improper things.

Ethical business practice and following your company's code of conduct is critically important, no matter what profession you're in. Our credibility, integrity, and character are cornerstones for how we're viewed by others and our ethical behavior must always be maintained at the highest levels.

Whether you're a new entry-level employee or someone at a senior level, there will be times of stress and pressure to complete projects and achieve positive results for your company. That is just a part of your job. Those challenges can sometimes lead you to strategies or ideas that you know are pushing the limits of what's acceptable. The path from bending the proper codes of conduct to inching into behavior that could be considered unethical isn't that far. And then, some unethical behavior is dangerously close to being illegal.

Fortunately, the vast majority of us would never consider behavior or tactics that would jeopardize our reputation or our character. We recognize that, as business professionals, we must maintain the highest standards of integrity. That doesn't mean we won't encounter situations where we may see or hear about unprofessional conduct.

Always think twice if you think you may be pushing the limit; if necessary, ask your manager for assistance. There is also the simple exercise of being able to look at yourself in the mirror to know what's right or may be questionable. It's a simple and effective reality check.

EXCEL AND
SPREADSHEET
TRAINING

● ● ●

It's late in the day on a Friday, your finance liaison is at an offsite meeting, the department coordinator has left, and you're the last one in the office. A client from another time zone has just requested a rush proposal. Can you put together the required spreadsheet P&L, a few analyses, multiple comparative scenarios, and link the data to a few other worksheets? If you've got the experience with Excel, Google Sheets, or other spreadsheet software, then good for you, and move on to the next entry.

Many software applications have changed over the years or become obsolete. Database packages that I once used are now long gone. Spreadsheet software from the early days like VisiCalc, and then later, Lotus 1-2-3 have faded from most memories. However, Microsoft Excel is still more than relevant in most businesses for basic and even more complex financial spreadsheet reviews.

Through the years when I'd interview people, I'd always ask about their ability to work with spreadsheets. The answers covered the gamut and, even today, I still hear a wide range of explanations of why people can or cannot do it.

You need to have a working capability for whatever programs your company uses for forecasting, budgeting, and other financial work. For many departments, Excel is used and then linked to some other corporate program or CRM. There are courses probably offered through your human resources department, books, and some great online classes on sites like LinkedIn Learning.

Do you need to be a certified Excel user? No, unless you're in the finance department. However, I don't care if you're in sales, marketing, business development, or another function, you need to know how to create a spreadsheet with formulas, analysis, prepare a simple pivot table, and be able to link to cells from other worksheets. Sign up for a refresher class today.

EXHIBITING EMPATHY AND COMPASSION ARE VALUABLE SKILLS

● ● ●

There's an old saying about treating people as you would want to be treated. When we're feeling low or we're feeling good, we've had some disappointments, or we've had some successes, how do you feel when someone takes the time to ask you how you're doing? I don't mean the toss-away line, "Hey, how are ya?" I mean when they look at you in the eyes and truly ask how things are going or show positive feedback when you're celebrating an accomplishment. Don't you feel good when someone has taken the time to care?

Now, think back to the last time you did this for someone else. For many people, this comes as second-nature, while other people find it awkward to reach out and express their feelings. It's a much easier thing to do when you're celebrating someone's success but you need to make sure you mean it when you say congratulations or cheers. It can be more diffi-cult, though, to reach out to someone when the person is ill, lost a loved one, or lost a job. I've been amazed through the years, watching and listening to see how some people handle those situations. You'll spot some people make a sharp turn in the hallway to avoid contact with an impacted colleague. You may even hear them explain with embarrassed hesitation, "I just don't know what to say to them," and they avoid communicating at all.

Again, some people are very good at expressing sympathy but I'm referring to empathy and compassion. Empathy is defined as the feeling that you understand and share another person's experiences and emotions. Compassion is showing and expressing concern for someone else's adversity. It can be done verbally and, if expressing yourself is difficult, it's the ability to show a caring or understanding expression or, when appropriate, a subtle touch of the arm or hand.

Exhibiting compassion and having empathy just doesn't happen and you have to work at it, practice it, and make a conscious decision to do it. You need to recognize it, do it, and mean it. When that happens, the true care you show to others pays back dividends in so many ways and will make you a better colleague, leader, business professional, and, most importantly, a better person.

EXPENSE ACCOUNTS

• • •

Expense accounts can be a great thing and they can be very dangerous too. In the course of my career, I've seen more than a few people get in trouble because they didn't handle their business expenses properly.

Understanding the proper use of your expenses, the approval process, and reimbursement all starts with your company policy. No one spends a lot of time reading through the corporate documents on your portal, but given the seriousness of the subject, you need to. What you did at a prior employer or how it was handled in a different division doesn't apply to the job you're in now. Every company handles expenses differently and some companies are much stricter than others. Quite simply, you must adhere to your company's current policy.

The next step is getting on the same page with your manager. Again, it doesn't matter what your last manager used to say about entertainment spending or if your old boss was very lenient about submitting expense reports. What matters is who you report to now and the direction they give with travel and entertainment use. Depending on your job function, at the start of the fiscal year, you'll get a budget for expenses. Every manager I ever had was pretty firm about not wanting me to exceed that expense number. Going past that number is a big red flag that is visible to many people at your employer. Believe me, you don't want to be the person who blows away the T&E expense line.

After that, much of the policy depends on your job and your industry. For some jobs, entertaining buyers, accounts, or clients is, in many ways, a part of the business. It's expected and if you look around a restaurant at lunch or dinner, you're not the only businessperson there.

Let's look at three expense categories:

- Lunches & Dinners: There was joke about me in my old company from years ago where I got more than bit irked when I heard some of the staff had taken a customer out to dinner and everyone ordered whole lobsters. Lobsters? Give me a break. Like I said before, you have to know your manager and his style.

- Hotels & Airlines: I follow the same philosophy about spending as though it was my own personal checking account. When I travel, I like staying in nice rooms, but I'm sorry, the top-of-the-line hotel can't be in the cards. Most companies have really strict airline policies. Unless you're taking a long overseas flight, don't assume you can fly business or first class.

- Events & Entertainment: An afternoon of golf, a concert at the arena, or a massage at the spa. These are pretty common charges in some industries and can really push the conduct limits. Be sure you're double-checking before booking any of these services

Reputation, credibility, and your personal integrity can be jeopardized if you abuse your expenses. Repairing that damage is extremely difficult, if not impossible. I've got a pretty straight-forward test you can do on your own if you're wondering whether your spending is appropriate or has some ethical question marks. Look at yourself in mirror and ask yourself those questions. If you think you might be pushing it a bit, you are! Think twice.

FAMILY COMES FIRST

• • •

At the end of the day, what really matters? I think we all need to ask ourselves that question every so often and, for some people, even more frequently. We all have different priorities, goals for our careers, and varying beliefs on what we want to achieve.

I learned in my thirties that I would be missing out on so many things if I put my work in front of my family. There were times when I was on an airplane and didn't make it back for a school event or game on the ballfield. However, more often than not, I was able to adjust my travel or shorten a meeting at the home office to ensure I was at family activities in time. There are events that only occur once, so missing them can really mean a lost opportunity and memory. It can also have a negative impact on other family members.

Every so often, we read about certain industries or specific jobs where the work days can reach fourteen hours or more and weekends are consumed with preparing reports. That can happen in any profession every so often, but if that's the norm, don't you think you need to reconsider what you could be missing? Is that what life's all about?

Some people thrive on the demands of their job. That said, I believe we all need to prioritize our families' needs' first and then those of our jobs. Some food for thought.

FIRE IN THE BELLY

● ● ●

There have been a number of times during the course of my career when I really loved what I was doing. I worked with some fantastic people who not only were exceptional professionals, but enjoyable to be around as well. Business was great, the markets were expanding, and it was a lot of fun to go to work every day.

Frankly, what I've come to appreciate is that it's an experience that not everyone gets to enjoy with their work. It's called having "Fire in the Belly," where your determination, drive, and energy to perform at the best of your ability are fully engaged. Nothing is ever perfect, but when you're running at 90 percent efficiency and effectiveness, you feel that you and your team are invincible. It also means you're really loving what you're doing.

Try to find an opportunity like that during your career. Experiencing that fire in your belly is amazing and so rewarding.

FIRST IMPRESSIONS DO MAKE A DIFFERENCE

• • •

A few years ago, one of the sales managers I worked with was interviewing a prospective candidate for a sales territory slot in our company. It happened to be a day I was dressed casually, since I wasn't seeing customers and I wasn't planning to interview anyone. I was at a coffee shop across the street when a man in front of me was rather rude with the cashier and, when I told him politely to take it easy, he wasn't happy me with either. Later that morning, I got a call from that sales manager saying he had met a great candidate and, since time was a factor, he hoped I could alter my schedule and see him. Well, you know where this is going, right? I was in my office when the sales manager brought in the very confident and smiling prospective recruit whose demeanor changed quickly when I asked, "How was your coffee?"

That's a true story and extreme example, but the reality is the first impression we make when meeting someone new is often a lasting one and, if you give a poor first impression, it can take a number of subsequent meetings, if at all, to alter the view you've created.

As businesspeople, we're often in situations where we're meeting new people, whether it's a one-on-one session or a group presentation to three, six, ten, or more decisionmakers.

If you don't think we're being evaluated and judged as soon as we walk into the room, then you're sorely mistaken.

There are a number of factors that impact a first impression but, most importantly, you need to be authentic. Don't try and fake it; just be yourself. When I'm meeting new people, there are five key things that trigger first impressions for me and, from experience, I know most businesspeople would agree.

1. Do you smile when you meet someone? Is the smile real or fake? A warm, honest smile is a great way to start.
2. Do you shake hands firmly? Too strong or too weak?
3. I've meet people whose body language was so poor, either with posture or with "attitude" when I've met them that I knew right away we were off to bad start.
4. Eye contact is an important factor for me and I expect it from people I meet. A buyer can access your confidence very quickly if you divert your eyes a lot.
5. Attire is another key factor in the process of developing a first impression and it's a tough one. You really need to give thought to whom you're meeting with and the company too. For me, I always err on the side of overdressing, especially when meeting a new potential client.

Developing a strong first impression takes practice. It may feel awkward, but experiment by looking at yourself in front of a mirror. Check out your smile, see if you can maintain eye contact, observe your posture, and work to create a warm, positive, and confident look. Don't be shy; Consider asking a friend or colleague to give some feedback.

So, spend the time to work on and improve the first impression you make. Small, subtle changes can make such a big difference.

FOSTER GOOD
WORKING
RELATIONSHIPS

● ● ●

Being realistic whenever you're working in a group of more than a few people is essential because there's no way that everyone is always going to get along. That's actually good news because you need diversity in personality, style, and beliefs to generate new ideas and creativity. Fostering good working relationships doesn't mean everyone smiles, agrees, and supports each other with positive feedback. Instead, strive for an atmosphere where people respect each other enough to realize that some conflict is healthy, new ideas should be debated, and everyone has a voice at the table.

Fostering a good working relationship touches on so many positive qualities. Along with trust, I think it is supporting others' development, providing encouragement and motivation, and doing that in an open and honest environment. This then leads to stronger teamwork, collaboration, and a corporate culture of a productive work setting.

Those who can actively be a part of fostering a business situation like this often have strong people skills, emotional intelligence, and are excellent communicators. They become managers who are respected, are often innovators, and, most certainly, find the path to leading others. Always strive to improve your ability to foster stronger working relationships.

GET AWAY FROM YOUR DESK

● ● ●

Getting up and away from your desk and work station is important advice, no matter what your job is. You can't be tied to your desk from nine to five and expect to be productive, creative, and, most importantly, healthy. Saying that you get up and walk to go to meetings and stroll to the lunch room doesn't make it any better. If your job is one that could be totally work station-based, like in finance or creative, you have to set aside time to get away and refresh your mind.

I once worked with a senior executive in finance and, every day, he would leave the office for fifteen to twenty minutes and take a walk away from the building. For me, I would often just walk around the building. Along with clearing my head, it gave me the opportunity to give quick greetings to colleagues in other departments. Whatever you choose, initiate a plan to get away from your desk.

If you're in sales, marketing, business development, or any customer-facing position and you're finding yourself spending too many hours in your office, then shame on you. You've let your tasks dictate your mission rather than you focusing on the goals and objectives for which you were hired. At times in my career, I suddenly became an administrator rather someone who was supposed to be out in the marketplace. Thankfully, I recognized it early on and would say, "I have to get out of here and see clients/customers/accounts."

Never let your job tie you down. Take the necessary steps to make sure you get away from your desk.

GIVING
CONSTRUCTIVE
CRITICISM

● ● ●

Maybe we should start this entry with, "Were you asked to give constructive criticism or are you offering it up without being prompted?" There's a big difference, although, in both circumstances, you need to handle it delicately and professionally. The skill of being able to read your audience is so important when you're offering constructive criticism. You need to be able to sense when you've struck a nerve or maybe are a bit too honest for what the other person cares to hear.

You have to remember that when people say they're open to hearing some constructive criticism, the receptiveness can vary dramatically, depending on the individual.

An effective way to give criticism is to soften any negatives with a positive. It's called "sandwiching." It's pretty self-explanatory and, visually, you can imagine how that looks. After you give critical advice, you "sandwich" it with something more upbeat before going back to the next piece of critical advice.

I think the concept of "less is more" also applies. When giving feedback, don't overwhelm the person until you're able to assess their reactions. Offer your views in small doses before giving out more.

No matter how hard we try, we all get a bit defensive sometimes. It's our work, we've tried hard, and now we're getting criticism that we weren't expecting. If you're the one giving the feedback, I think it's also as important to recommend how something can be improved or offer up ideas for ways of making it better. My defensive mechanism has often been, "Okay, I understand what you're saying. What should I have done?" If I get some ideas, then I'm much more willing to accept the constructive criticism.

Remember, gauge your audience, read their eyes, check their mannerisms, and be in tune with how they respond. By doing so, you can reinforce the word "constructive" so it positions the criticism in a positive way.

GLOBAL MEETINGS— RESPECT TIME ZONES

• • •

There are so many companies today that are global, with offices in cities around the world. It's very common to have regular conference calls between New York and London or Tokyo and San Francisco.

I'm a bit surprised when I talk with friends and colleagues from various offices around the world and they tell me they have meetings at the strangest hours. If you have important meetings with global colleagues, I think we all should expect the occasional meeting at some awful hour. However, a regularly scheduled meeting at 10:00 p.m. or 5:30 a.m.? That's just not right.

If you work globally, you need to know global time zones. If it's 8:00 p.m. in London, then it's 3:00 p.m. in New York, 12:00 p.m. in San Francisco, 7:00 a.m. in Melbourne, and 1:30 a.m. in New Delhi. Having a regular global conference call with all locations participating live is impossible unless you're not respecting your coworkers. An afternoon meeting from New York? Where does that work?

Keep a chart handy on your computer with the times of your global offices. Do you know the twenty-four-hour "military time" clock too? The world doesn't revolve around New York, London, or San Francisco.

GLOBAL WORK AND CROSS-CULTURAL COMPETENCY

• • •

One of the aspects of my job in sales that I've enjoyed the most has been working with colleagues and customers from around the world. I've often said that the obstacles and opportunities along with the struggles and excitement are things we experience, no matter where we live. We may speak different languages but the smile you show and the great feeling you have after closing a sale is a bond that breaks down all barriers.

That being said, I've also seen how as businesspeople working across borders can be a delicate process too. A businessperson from the U.S. working with a client from Singapore is a lot different than working with a client from New York. I've seen ignorance and awkward situations arise when people haven't taken the time to learn about customs, culture, and ethical behavior in countries they may be visiting. This quickly separates the inexperienced businessperson from the one who has taken the time to learn and earn the respect from their counterparts.

Planning, preparation, research, and asking questions are so critical before even venturing into a setting outside of your own country. The important aspect of knowing your audience is the key advice.

Through the years, I've found that there are a number of seemingly insignificant things that occur during a business meeting that are handled differently depending on the country you're in. Here are a few that come to mind:

- Greetings, Handshakes, Touching: My tendencies have always been to be a very upbeat greeter, hand-shaker, and if I see someone I know well, I do give a hug. Even in the U.S., I know I need to tone it down with certain people I meet. However, globally, I'm much more reserved in certain countries. There are also religions where my practice of a subtle touch on the arm would be considered rude. A hug? No way is that proper.
- Meeting Etiquette: This is a really interesting one since it does vary from industry to industry and from country to country. Protocol is the rule in some cases where you'll find that the most senior person in the room is deferred to first and speaking up before them would be an insult. In some cultures, people don't speak and offer their views unless they're asked. That's why it's so important to do your research first. You'll know the times to sit back and wait, along with when you'll want to gently ease people into the conversation.
- Gifts: To offer a gift or not. It's always sensitive and always worth double-checking. In some parts of the world a small gesture of a gift is expected while in other countries it would be totally unethical.
- Dinners and Entertainment: Similar to gifting, how you entertain or not is something you need to be very clear about. A formal tone is expected in some cultures. In others, my style of telling jokes and stories would be frowned upon.

The rule is: do your research. Ask for guidance before you travel abroad to work with customers. Speak with your local contacts and be honest. Tell them you want to make sure you're following proper conduct and not doing anything that might be construed as unethical.

Our businesses are more and more global in this day and age. It's critical that you learn and understand the local culture and customs so you'll avoid any embarrassing misunderstandings. This is an investment that all smart business professionals make to ensure they're always working ethically and properly.

GOALS AT WORK

● ● ●

Setting goals is a project that I believe is critically important to do, both for our business and personal lives. They provide with you something important to strive for and also require you to develop a plan and a strategy for how to achieve each goal. I've seen people have long lists of goals, but I believe smaller, more manageable ones are better.

There is an outstanding model for setting goals called SMART and I would recommend it highly. I've researched this in a variety of places and SMART was first written about in a 1981 issue of the Management Review. The title of the article was, "There's a S.M.A.R.T. Way to Write Management Goals and Objectives." It was written by George Doran, Arthur Miller, and James Cunningham.

S—Specific: Oftentimes, we're not focused with our goals. By being specific you clearly define the areas needed for improvement.

M—Measurable: These are the key performance indicators, targets, or anything that would be an indication of progress. You're tracking your goal.

A—Assignable: You, a colleague, or your team needs to own the goal. You're responsible for it.

R—Realistic: There's nothing more demoralizing and motivation-killing than to have a goal that is virtually impossible to achieve. You want to stretch with the bar set high, but you want to able to realistically reach the summit too.

T—Time Related: I'm a believer in timetables, dates, and deadlines for most projects I'm involved with. With a goal, you need to have some timeline for accomplishing it or else you run the risk of it languishing and becoming a negative.

I think goals are so necessary and a great tool for self-improvement along with growth for your team and company. Along with SMART, remember not to overcomplicate them, make sure that they are focused, and see them as a positive way build your business and yourself.

HARASSMENT AND
DISCRIMINATION

● ● ●

It's unfortunate that harassment and discrimination of one form or another continues to be a news topic in the media. You would think that everyone would have gotten the message by now, but sadly that is not the case. It's not limited to specific industries, locations, or professions. The problem is one that shows no boundaries.

Harassment and discrimination include everything from unwanted sexual advances and verbal abuse to bias based on sexual orientation, religion, race, or disability. There are many forms and each are hurtful and painful for the victims.

The days of this should be behind us, but they are not. The reports of companies turning the other cheek, offering second chances, or covering up can no longer be tolerated either. An employee saying that he was just kidding or didn't mean it that way is not an excuse.

As a manager, a leader, or a colleague of a co-worker, everyone must be aware that there is no leeway on any form of discrimination or harassment. Companies and leadership must to be firm on this during the onboarding of new staff and during more frequent corporate conduct policy training. The training and policy must be explicit, clear, and direct.

If you are the victim of harassment or discrimination, it's very easy for me to say, "Speak up and seek help immediately." It should be able to happen that way. However, it can be a very stressful and even painful experience to take that action. Seek guidance from a trusted person on how best to handle your specific situation.

HAVE PATIENCE

• • •

Dictionary.com defines patience as, "an ability or willingness to suppress restlessness or annoyance when confronted with delay. It's the quality of being patient, as the bearing of provocation, annoyance, misfortune, or pain, without complaint, loss of temper, irritation, or the like."

I've chosen a few examples for you to think of how you would handle these situations or if they sound familiar to you.

You're at a stoplight and the light turns green, but driver in the car ahead of you has her head down and is clearly texting. How many seconds will it take before you hit your horn?

We've all spotted this person in front of the gate agent at the airport. The boarding hasn't started and there's an individual complaining that there's no new update about why the plane is delayed.

The instructions are to call an 800-number for more assistance and you get then trapped in, "Our menu options have changed." Then, when you finally reach the right department, you're number thirty-five in line, but, "Your call is important to us." How long do you stay on the line?

It's the hottest new restaurant in town, but it doesn't take reservations. The hostess or host tells you that it will be about thirty minutes before you will be seated. It's now been forty-five minutes.

We've become a society that expects deliveries within forty-eight hours, immediate answers to questions we submit online to customer service departments, and our patience levels have become almost unrealistically low. Some people are so much better with this than others. They're able to take a breath and recognize that things often just take more time. Others of us need to be reminded of that. I'm reminding you now.

HELP PEOPLE OUT
WHEN THEY'VE
LOST A JOB

● ● ●

This is one of those perplexing things that I've noticed many times over the years. A colleague loses a job, he then sends notes to friends and former co-workers asking for assistance, and the responses or lack of feedback are astounding. I really don't understand why this happens but it's more common than you would expect.

When people lose jobs or are looking for the next opportunity, outplacement firms and career coaches have a standard recommendation. Network, network, network. It really is the best advice and the instructions are to reach out to former coworkers, your LinkedIn connections, and personal business contact list. When I work with coaching clients, I now add a qualifier and say that you shouldn't be surprised or disappointed when you don't hear back from everyone.

I'm far from being a psychologist or sociologist, but there's a similar phenomenon that happens in an office environment when someone is dismissed. There are some people who reach out to console, while others hide. When some of your connections get that email asking for assistance or career advice, a few respond but the majority don't. I'm sure there's a study somewhere about human nature and situations like this.

Instead of shrugging and feeling you don't know what to say or reading the email, feeling bad, and not responding, reach out and show some empathy. You may not have any ideas, or don't have any job leads. Be honest and say that. Tell them you feel for them, will keep your eyes open, and will alert them if you hear anything. That's 100 percent better than looking the other way or letting an email sit unanswered.

HONOR YOUR COMMITMENTS— DON'T MAKE PROMISES YOU CAN'T KEEP

● ● ●

If you want to be an exceptional businessperson and earn the respect and the trust of your colleagues and peers, you have to honor the commitments you've given. This aligns closely with your "work ethic" and, "being honest." Quite simply, if you say you're going to do something by a certain date, then you must honor that commitment. That doesn't seem to be an unrealistic thing to expect, does it?

In your career or in personal life, have you ever come across a person who says he'll provide information, or agrees to participate in a group task, or promises to show up at a specific time for a meeting or event? When he doesn't, you get annoyed, frustrated, and, in some cases, you'll get angry. Obviously, a mistake can happen to any one of us, but if it happens regularly from a person, then I guarantee you keep that in your memory. Not honoring your commitments can label you as unreliable, unprofessional, and untrustworthy. Your coworkers could think of you as unsupportive, not a team player, and even selfish. Those are hard labels to shake and, once your reputation is tarnished, it can take a long time to repair, if ever.

Sometimes we agree do to things for fear that if we don't say yes, then we'll be viewed as weaker or not as prepared as our other colleagues. I know I've had times when I've said, "Yes, I can do that project," or, "Sure, I'll attend that weekly one-hour meeting and present on this subject or whatever." Then, as my work builds up with other commitments, regular responsibilities, and tasks I feel myself getting overwhelmed, not performing at the level I should be, getting stressed, and working extra time so that I can keep the promises and commitments.

I believe that, in business (personal life, too), honoring commitments is paramount. If you say you're going to do something by a certain date, then unless there are extreme circumstances preventing that from happening, then that date is set in stone.

It can happen when commitments may not be able to be met and we get in situations where timelines get delayed, deliveries may get impacted, or you're unable to be at an important meeting or supply your team with the information you had promised. You can fall into a trap digging a deeper hole by giving excuses, asking for a few more days, or, worse yet, saying nothing. That leads to the dreaded "bad news surprise" that can happen and be an awful experience for everyone. Being upfront and honest is always the best approach.

In business, our reputations and the trust we earn from our clients, customers, and colleagues is worth everything. It is almost impossible to recover from the loss of trust. Be the person who can be depended on and can always be trusted.

HOW DO YOU
SOUND TO OTHERS?
LISTEN TO YOUR
VOICE

● ● ●

Do you remember the first time you heard your voice from a recorder or watched yourself speak on video? It can often be a real surprise and, that initial time, you may ask, "Do I really sound like that?"

It is a good idea to evaluate how you sound since that's how others in business settings hear you, understand the point you're making, and, in some cases, how they evaluate you. You might have a thick accent from a certain region of the country or are from another country and it makes it difficult for people to understand you. Changing this would probably require you to take some special speech training.

However, there are a number of characteristics that you can work on by yourself and, over time, make some significant improvements.

    Speed: If you speak really fast, you can sound hyper and those you're communicating with can't keep up with you. Your message is lost and you may even hear people say, "Phew," when you complete your thought. Conversely, speak too slowly and you'll see people fidget, drop eye contact, and show a total lack of interest. Proper pacing with our speech is more important than you may suspect.

○ Volume: Have you ever been in a meeting when someone speaks so softly that you have to lean forward just to hear the person? What about the colleague who speaks so loudly that he sounds like a drill sergeant? There are times when speaking at varying volume levels can be a great way of making a point. However, consistently speaking too quietly or too loudly will end up distracting people in a potentially negative way.

○ Enunciation: When you let your voice die mid word or just don't speak clearly, your message can come out incorrectly or be misinterpreted. Poor enunciation can occur if you're tired or if your interest level has waned. You need to work on this, and a great way to monitor it is by looking at yourself in a mirror. Stand up straight, take a deep breath, and see if your lips moving. Make sure you're including the endings to words to sound more professional. Are you saying "selling" and "going" or "sellin'" and "goin'"?

Monitoring your voice and speech patterns may not be something you've considered but it really is very important. It's something you can correct and improve very quickly with practice too.

HOW TO LIST NAMES
ON A GROUP EMAIL
AND THE USE OF
BLIND COPIES

● ● ●

Years ago, I sent an email out to about ten people and I randomly listed the names as they came to my mind. Later that day, a colleague who was on that email list came to me and asked why his name was listed last. I didn't know what was going on until he said he should be listed first, since his title was most senior. I was so dumbfounded that I just nodded, said okay, and walked away. Later on, I thought of so many better responses that I really should have said. You can easily eliminate that problem by just alphabetizing your addresses. It is advice that I've followed for years.

Sending group emails using the blind copy (Bcc) approach can also be effective tool. It is a great way to send a group message to a lot of people and it prevents someone mistakenly replying to all, since that response can't be done. This is prefect for announcements or general messages and what makes using a Bcc such a good tool.

The opposite is true when you're sending an email directly to one, two, or dozens of people and Bcc someone. It can be so dangerous. Why? It can only cause a problem and, in the long run, can only hurt you. I remember a manager once getting blind carbon copied on an email and he forwarded to someone else, who contacted by mistake the people on the original email. It created quite the amount of ill will and a lot of damage control was required. The lesson: never use a Bcc for this purpose.

IMPORTANCE OF A STRONG WORK ETHIC

● ● ●

This may expose me as an old-fashioned manager, but I'm a big believer in having a strong work ethic.

There are times when you may hear someone say, "Wow, isn't it amazing how this person seems to get all the breaks? He's always so lucky." Or, "How come that person always seems to be in the right place at the right time when something good happens?" It may have happened when some new business developed, a big deal was closed, or when an exciting new position in the company opened up.

There are times when luck does play a part of things or good fortune seems to shine on some people more than others but, in the long run, the odds don't work that way. The reality is success follows those who work hard, are committed to doing their best, and don't sit back waiting for things to happen but, instead, they act.

Taking action, working hard, and having the work ethic to fully commit yourself to a job or responsibility should be automatic; Don't you think? Unfortunately, in my career I've seen more than a few times when people try to cut corners, don't give 100 percent, and don't fully engage themselves to be successful for their companies and themselves.

Maybe it's old-fashioned to expect people to show up to work on time, not adding an extra fifteen minutes to a break or thirty minutes more to lunch or be the first one out the door when the work day ends. The reality is it's the effort you give that matters, not the amount of time at your desk or doing other parts of your job. However, you need you ask yourself if your work habits are playing a role in the success you may or may not be having at work.

Every so often, it's worth evaluating our work habits and refining them as necessary to ensure that we're performing to the best of our abilities. We each have our most productive times of the day and it's an excellent idea to make sure we're focused on handling our most important work during the times of the day when we're at our peak productivity levels. At the end of the day, it all comes down to the results generated but I think your chances for success are a lot better if you take the steps to put yourself in favorable positions.

It's that basic commitment to taking action and having a work ethic that creates success and you will be surprised at how often good things will happen when you follow that path. There's a lot of truth to what my first manager would say, "Success just doesn't happen, you have to work hard, take action, and you have to go out and earn it."

IMPROVE YOUR
WRITING SKILLS

● ● ●

We've all become experts at writing quick text messages, doing social media posts with just hashtags on Instagram, and using abbreviations or acronyms for everything. In our companies, we've learned the art of using four to five-word bullet points so they fit nicely on one line for our PowerPoint presentations.

However, "IMHO," what's now happened is that our skills for writing clear and effective business correspondence has waned dramatically. Having said that, each year for decades, you will find an article somewhere that college professors are saying that the writing ability for incoming freshmen has never been worse. So maybe I sound like an old businessman with a similar issue as the college professor teaching the Intro 101 course. It's actually a positive thing that we're writing more succinctly and realizing that emails longer than a few sentences just aren't read. Long-winded written commentary just doesn't work.

There are times when strong writing skills are necessary. You can easily separate the good communicators from those who are woefully ineffective and, in some cases, unprofessional. Executive summaries, strategic plans, and presentations are just a few examples of documents that need special care. It's true for emails too, and don't forget about your entries in your company CRM such as Salesforce. You will stand out for all of the wrong reasons if you can't construct your correspondence at a professional level.

One of the best courses I took in college was on business and report writing. The professor was incredibly tough, the best grade she gave was a "B", but the lessons have lasted a lifetime. If you've never taken a writing course, you must, and if it's been a while, you should go for a refresher. I would urge you to sign up for a course that's often offered through corporate learning and development departments. If that's not available, look at programs at local community colleges or continuing education classes.

While you're at it, dust off your spellchecker and be sure to use it. It's also a good time to learn the proper times to use: their/there/they're, to/too/two, accept/except, you're/your, and other words often misused.

The way you write, use proper grammar, and spell can make quite the positive or negative impression.

IS THERE SUCH
A THING AS
CONFIDENTIAL?

• • •

Confidential means that it's for your eyes or ears only. It's information that must not be shared unless you've been given approval by the sender. If you break this assurance, then in my view, your credibility and trustworthiness are tarnished. To me, it's a reflection on your character when you spread or leak confidential information.

Through the years, I've come to realize that confidential information rarely stays confidential for long. Once you share even a snippet of detail with one person, chances are the news will spread widely pretty quickly.

The forwarding of emails marked confidential should never happen but it does. I remember, years ago, I wrote a note about a sensitive business subject that was marked confidential. A few weeks later, I got a call from a business newspaper reporter asking me about the note. Needless to say, I was flabbergasted, but learned a valuable lesson. The ironic twist was that, a few years later, I mentioned the story to a colleague who said, "Well confidentially, here are the names of the people who gave your email to that reporter."

"Confidential" should mean exactly that. Don't share it, don't spread word of it, and if you have classified information, be mindful that, at some point, it will become public.

IT'S OKAY TO ASK FOR HELP

● ● ●

Some people never ask for assistance and often wait too long to request some help. They always believe they can fix things themselves, they don't want to bother others, or they are afraid to admit they need assistance.

To some degree, could it be a lack of confidence? Asking for help means to me that you're willing to learn, be coached, and know your limitations. You're not afraid to raise your hand and say that you could use a little support or assistance.

There have been instances when I've worked with people whose intentions were actually good-hearted in that they didn't want to bother anyone. They struggled to find an answer, complete a project, or worse yet, solve a problem without asking for help. The end result was a bigger mess that should have been addressed much sooner.

In some companies, the atmosphere is so stressful and toxic that people are afraid to ask for any assistance because they fear others will look down on them. Those are companies that you should avoid.

Not asking for help early enough puts you at risk for potentially having to tell your manager you've got a "surprise." (See the entry, "Don't Hold Back from Telling Bad News.") It really is okay to ask for help, it's the smart thing to do, and in my mind, is a sign of confidence.

JARGON, BUZZWORDS, AND ANNOYING PHRASES

● ● ●

"It's probably very important that we all have our ducks in a row to leverage the core values that we empower to those on the SWAT team who drink the corporate Kool-Aid because it really is what it is. I also want to give you a heads-up that we may need to take this offline because I have a hard stop."

That may be an extreme example of two sentences with jargon and annoying phrases, but we all know people who spout statements that may not be too far off from these kinds of sentences. It can be an easy habit to fall into and we all have times when a catchphrase becomes a too-regular part of our vocabulary. It may seem harmless at first but, over time, it can really turn others off, will be annoying to hear, and, ultimately, diminish the value of the point you're trying to get across. Accomplished and effective businesspeople are those who are aware of what they're saying and how it is perceived by others.

The other area that I have always found to be a problem are those people who use buzzwords or acronyms and just assume everyone knows what they mean. For example, "The DBM will be investing in CRM for the NAM's and AE's starting in FY 20." In English, this means the divisional business manager will be investing in customer relationship management software for the national account managers and account executives starting in fiscal year 2020. This assumption that people know what you're saying happens in all companies. You always should pay special attention to ensure you're being clear when you use any acronyms, especially the first time you say or use them in written copy.

KEEP THINGS SIMPLE

● ● ●

Keeping things simple sounds so practical, really smart, and just plain commonsense. Yet how many meetings have you attended or presentations have you read and, when finished, you wondered, "Why are we making this so complicated?" It's like having a regular standing meeting each week that's an hour in length and then using the full hour each week, even though you may not need the full hour. In business, we often fall guilty to adding more content, more agenda items, and more discussion because we either think we should or the time is available to do it.

I used to nod my head in agreement at the acronym, K.I.S.S.—Keep It Simple Stupid—since it very clearly makes a direct point. In writing this book, I found out some of the history about where it was first stated. From a variety of sources, I learned that it came from the US Navy and when they would talk about systems. They believed they worked best when they were simple and not complicated. BusinessDictionary.com defines KISS as: "A term which simply indicates that the simplest solution or path should be taken in a situation." This principle can be applied to any scenario, including many business activities, such as planning, management, and development."

Many years ago, I read a book called, *The Power of Simplicity* by Jack Trout. The subtitle is, *A Management Guide to Cutting through the Nonsense of Doing Things Right*" It was one of the better twenty-dollar investments I made for myself. The focus of the book taught me a lot about the importance of common sense in making business decisions. The four key take-aways are: Fight Complexity, Embrace Simplicity, Be a Contrarian, and Respect your People.

Keeping things simple isn't easy because often we are faced with business issues that are complicated. However, always remember that making decisions and K.I.S.S are what can separate the successful businessperson from the bureaucrat.

KEEP YOUR EGO IN CHECK

● ● ●

Most successful business professionals believe in themselves and have developed their self-confidence to a strong level. However, you need to be aware that self-confidence doesn't mean you need to tell everyone how great you are, what an exceptional manager you may be, or how your department is performing better than all of the others.

The most confident leaders, the most admired peers, and the most accomplished businesspeople are the ones who have confidence in themselves and let their results or actions do the talking. They don't need to stand up and toot their own horn, so to speak, or wave their arms extolling their successes. The humility that they show earns them even greater respect. The confident person rarely says "I"; instead they openly encourage others with genuine enthusiasm and they keep their ego in check.

I once worked with someone who was just really good at his job. He didn't need to be overly vocal to let us know how well he was doing with his sales. We all could spot the results in our weekly reports. However, he was a "know-it-all" and, each week, they made a habit of letting us know how successful he was. To make it worse, he would give us the details of how he accomplished it. I used to count the number of times he said the word "I" in a presentation and it became a running joke he didn't know about. Instead of being a team player, he was only out for himself and, I must confess, there were times that we would root against him. Someone with a large ego can quickly find himself isolated, not connected to the team, not respected, and often not rewarded with promotions or increased responsibilities.

Contrast that with the CEO of a company where I once worked. He never spoke about his personal successes but rather always made a point of highlighting accomplishments of those around him, from the entry-level person to his chief operating officer. He was confident, his ego was managed, and he rarely, if ever, acted, as if he wasn't a part of the team. This skill made him an even stronger leader, motivator, and someone we wanted to follow. It made for an exceptional combination of leadership and authenticity.

Being aware of yourself, understanding how people perceive you, and watching for signals from those you work with is a critical skill to learn. That is so true for ego. Believe in yourself, be confident in your skills and work performance, but let your results and achievements speak for themselves. Your peers and good managers will reward you with the much-deserved compliments when they are due. Keeping your ego balanced is way to focus on your team rather than individual success and, in the long run, makes you a better colleague and definitely a better leader.

KEEP YOUR HOME OFFICE WELL-ORGANIZED AND PROFESSIONAL

● ● ●

When I first became a sales representative, my home office was set up in a part of my apartment where I lived. I was single at time and my accommodations were modest, to say to least. It actually looked like I lived in an office. There were products I was selling all over the place, marketing materials stacked up on the floor, and sales printouts on a coffee table.

My sales manager came to work with me at one point and, after we had made some customer visits, we went back to my home office. He looked around at my setup and kept shaking his head. What he said next has stuck me to do this day, since it truly focuses on the importance of being a professional field sales representative. He looked at me and said, "Dean, you're managing a million-dollar territory for our company which is bigger than a number of local businesses here in town. You need to realize you're running a small business as field sales representative. You may be working out of your home, customers won't be coming over here, but you must treat this entire setup as the local face of our organization."

If you're a remote worker and you're in the process of setting up your home office, there are many factors you need to consider, especially if you're serious about viewing your work as running a small business. The list of items to consider is vast, but I'm going focus on three:

1. Office Layout: The story about my manager looking at my home office is a good reminder. You should design the layout of your office in the way you feel is most productive. I lean towards having the space fully separate from all other parts of my home. When you're on video calls, you want the background to look professional. I'd really be wary of files and product information all over the house. I'd also recommend keeping your laptop or desktop in one location, rather than using it on the kitchen table one day and in the family room the next day for consistency during video calls.

2. Communications: We've all experienced slow internet connections, mobile telephones suddenly disconnecting, and video conference calls with frozen faces. This is your business, so spend the money to have best connectivity possible. Purchase the better headset, microphone, and a video cam that has better quality than the one on your laptop and enables you to move around a bit. Try to be aware of barking dogs, lawn mowers, and kids arriving home from school.

3. Financial & Tax Implications: Your company's human resources department may be able to give guidance on these matters. Not only must you track your travel and business expenses to be properly reimbursed by your company, but other expenses such as personal use of your home for business may be deductible from federal and state tax returns. Don't assume, don't guess. Get advice from your personal accountant or seek a tax counselor.

You need to review the three items I have highlighted here and make sure you have a plan for each one that will make you feel comfortable. Then add others you feel are important and view this as though you're running your own small business.

KEEP YOUR TEMPER UNDER CONTROL

● ● ●

Combine stress, frustration, a lack of patience, and toss in some unrealistic expectations and there's a good chance that it won't take much for you to lose your temper. However, everyone has a different boiling point; some people fly off the handle at the slightest annoyance, while others have the ability to let things roll off their backs.

For years, I struggled with my temper. Most of the day, I'd be smiling and outgoing, but when I would get frustrated or lose my patience with someone or some issue, my temper would get the best of me. It may have felt productive for a minute or so, then you realize that you've done more damage than anything positive. That said, I would never use bad language, which takes losing your temper to an even worse level. I believe the use of inappropriate language is a line you can never cross without then experiencing serious consequences.

Losing your temper is rarely, if ever, a solution and recognizing that is the key. That was the critical thing I learned as I've tried to improve. Speaking up, defending your opinion, and being firm is okay. However, when you take it to the next level is when it becomes the real issue.

There are some important steps you can take if you find managing your temper a struggle at times. At the top of the list is: stop, take a breath, walk away, gather your thoughts, and regroup. You have to make a concerting effort to remember that. If it's an ongoing problem, seek some guidance from your human resources department, a coach, or a professional who can focus on your specific issues and patterns.

KEEP YOURSELF HONEST

● ● ●

I'd guess that it's probably true for all of us that, when we were very young, either our parents, our grandparents, some guardian or some teacher at school said in a very nice but firm voice, "You must always tell the truth and you must always be honest." Well, speaking for myself, I must admit I've had a few occasions where I may have strayed a bit. I think we all can be and are forgiven if we've had our moments where the truth may have been bent a bit. The fact is we are all human.

In business, your honesty and your integrity are the backbone of your reputation. Keeping yourself honest goes right to the core of your character, who you are as a person, and how others see you. In many evaluations or personal growth assessments, the aspect of ethics and honesty are often reviewed. I'd recommend paying close attention to that feedback to ensure you're being seen as nothing but trustworthy and honest by your managers and peers. A simpler approach is one I often will say to myself and to colleagues: "Can you look at yourself in the mirror and feel good about your actions or decisions?" If you can't, then you have some serious work to do.

Sometimes, with the stress and anxiety of doing our jobs, we may be tempted to say things to seemingly put us in a better light. The problem is it may work one time here and one time there, but, at the end of day, people will find out and the truth will be learned.

Unfortunately, far too often, we read about someone cheating a financial institution, a person involved with insider trading, or someone who has deceived a buyer. Those are the extreme cases but we all need to focus on our own work too. Honesty, integrity, and ethics—if you don't have that, then what do you have? Your reputation and how people view you is one of the most critical qualities you need to maintain in business. Tarnish it and it may be impossible to repair.

KNOW-IT-ALL AND THOSE WITH A POMPOUS ATTITUDE

● ● ●

We're all different and everyone has their own style and personality. It would be pretty boring and definitely a stagnate place to work if we all were exactly alike. Creativity would slow, conversations would be boring, and it would just be a bland business environment. That said, there are two types of people that seem to have a spot in every company and they can be pretty darn annoying.

Let me give you two examples of the type of person you just never want to be labeled as in your company. One is the "know-it-all." This is the person in every department meeting who feels as if he has to say something, no matter what the subject may be. To make matters worse, he is the self-proclaimed expert on everything too. This person informs everyone about articles he has read or makes references to research or studies he knows about. This leads then to the close relative of the, "know-it-all"—the person who takes it a step further and comes across as pompous too. "Yes, I know a lot about that subject, because during my MBA studies at "X" university, I wrote about it for major conference."

These people end up becoming isolated and are not invited to meetings or are overlooked for promotions. They fail to recognize their problem, either because of insecurity, ego, or being totally unaware of their audience and the negative impact they're having. Steer clear of these people at all costs, since they can drag you down and can be motivation killers.

KNOW YOUR AUDIENCE

● ● ●

There's a bit of advice that holds true for every profession and every situation, whether you're meeting with a new client, speaking in front an audience, or discussing a proposal with your boss. It's a simple phrase: know your audience.

So often we're anxious to get our message across or make our point that we forget what's really critical and what the reaction might be from others. We've spent all this time listening and being aware of our surroundings, but we've neglected to really think through what feedback we'll get. Or we've failed to put ourselves in the other person's position.

To me, knowing your audience is one of the most critical things to remember in business and my hope is it leaves a lasting impression on you. When I've done presentations, I've often shared a personal example that reinforces the importance of knowing your audience. It happened to me shortly after I was hired. My manager was an amazing trainer and mentor to me and he was also a religious person. He told me about his work for the church, how religious holidays meant a lot to him, and even when on the road, if it was a Sunday, he made sure to go to a service. He never pushed any more than that, but clearly, it was important to him.

A few months later as Christmas approached, I sent out cards to my friends, family, and some coworkers. It was a silly card with a bear on a pair of skies and I signed each card, "Have a Great Holiday, Deano"

ZIGGY © ZIGGY AND FRIENDS, INC.
Reprinted with permission of Andrews McMeel Syndication.

Nothing was offensive, but I didn't include any other message and it really was me just checking off the list, so to speak. Today, it would be the equivalent of sending a templatized "e" Christmas card. A day later, I got a card from my manager and it was of more religious tone, passing along blessings from the holiday and he added a paragraph or two of personal feedback about how much he liked working with me. I cringed when I saw his note and card, since I was so matter-of-fact with mine. A few weeks later, he smiled as he noted my card and said, "Way to know your audience, Dean."

Well, next Christmas, he sent my card back to me, adding a message, "Thinking of you." That had as much emotion as "Happy Holidays, Deano" message. The lesson of knowing your audience was clearly and delicately given to me and we've sent this card back and forth to each other for more than thirty years. We cross out the prior year's message and write it again every twelve months. It taught me something in a very fun and tangible way. I think it's pretty cool that we've done this for so long.

Successful businesspeople need to listen closely and be focused on what our colleagues, clients, or customers are telling us. We need to be aware of what things to avoid and what triggers positive responses from the people with whom we're meeting. We should be aware of our customer's interests, needs, and even personal beliefs and how that can have an impact on their decision-making. Knowing your audience is a skill that good businesspeople learn quickly.

KNOW YOUR COMPANY

● ● ●

This seems pretty obvious, but do you know the names and titles of all the senior management at your company? This would include everyone on the list of people who are on the executive team. The CEO, CFO, Division Head, Counsel, Chief Marketing Officer, and so on. If your company has a board of directors, it's also wise to know who those directors are too. You never know when you may come across one of them in the course of business or if one has a connection to help you with your job. I am actually pretty surprised that most people really don't have an awareness of who everyone is in their organization.

All companies produce documents to share with investors. If your company is publicly traded, there's a section on your website called Investor Relations. You'll find some great resources there that senior management uses to talk about the company to investors and analysts. It's an effective way to understand the key messages that management is communicating about your employer.

You'll also find annual reports, proxy statements, and other official documents that the SEC requires. These often have some really interesting tidbits of information. I'd also recommend you sign up to receive press releases that your company distributes. Many companies automatically email the big announcements to all employees but there are others that cover smaller deals or divisional news that may not be widely distributed.

Being on top of what's going on with all aspects of your company can not only be advantageous to you in managing your business, but also in enhancing your career. You'll have a better understanding of the direction senior leadership wants to take the company, so you can align your work to that overall mission too. Management will see that you are well informed and have taken the time to gain this knowledge.

KNOW YOUR COMPETITION

● ● ●

There are books, video courses, and classes on the subject of researching, monitoring, and knowing your competition. It's a subject that every successful businessperson realizes is important, yet for many, it is still not handled like a top priority. This entry obviously can't replace a course, but I've included it as firm reminder of the critical nature of knowing your competition.

There are hundreds of quotes about the subject such as, "Keep your friends close, but keep your competition closer." When you study your competition, learning their strengths and weaknesses, it can only make you a better businessperson and your company more successful.

Learning more about your competition is also an excellent way to increase collaboration within your company. Marketing, business development, finance, and sales can all work together to analyze specific aspects of a competitor's business. You could compile an endless list of things to track, but, in no special order, here are twelve.

1.   Pricing
2.   Strengths and Weaknesses
3.   Acquisitions and Investments
4.   New Hires and Recent Departures
5.   Social Media Efforts

6. Advertising Expenditures
7. New Product or Service Offerings
8. Discontinued Product or Serve Offerings
9. Stock Price
10. Investor Relations Presentations
11. Marketplace Feedback
12. Online Search Posts

Can you think of five more to add? Make this an ongoing priority for yourself and for your business. It can only make you more effective at your job.

KNOW YOUR CUSTOMERS

● ● ●

Whether you're in sales, marketing, business development, or any job within a company, you have to know everything you can about your customers. This is true even at the highest levels, when investor relations or corporate strategy meetings can distract executive team members. You can never lose sight that your customers drive your revenue and success.

This goes back to the critical process of planning, gathering information, and preparation before you even meet with you customer, client, or buyer. The framework would be very similar to doing to basic research project and then gathering the key facts, figures, and important information. This will give you a clearer picture about the customer and enables you to be so much better informed.

With companies, you can go to their websites and learn so much valuable information, especially from the "Investor Relations," "About Us," and "Corporate Information" sections. Before you meet with clients or buyers, you can do some online searches to see if they have done any presentations or written any articles. Pre-meeting searches on LinkedIn are commonplace now and expected, so you shouldn't be shy about reading background information there. It shows that you are doing your homework.

The most successful businesspeople listen closely and are focused on what their customers are telling them. You need to be aware of what things to avoid and what are the priorities for the people with whom you're meeting. Knowing your customers is an important skill that good businesspeople understand and learn quickly.

LEADERSHIP VS. MANAGEMENT

• • •

This is a common topic you will read about in business magazines and websites. There will be lots of comments and people chiming in with their ideas about the difference between leadership and management. While they are somewhat related, there is a big difference between the two.

I like this quote from Peter Drucker, who said, "Management is doing things right; leadership is doing the right thing."

It comes down to the fact that you follow good leaders, no matter who they are or where they are situated within an organization. They have what it takes to show vision, enable, motivate, and they model the way. It is a special quality often combined with charisma, where you look up to great leaders, respect, and trust them.

Your manager is someone is someone you work for and ensures that the process and the procedures function effectively and efficiently within your group or department. In essence, the manager assigns the objectives to get things completed successfully.

Not everyone can be an effective leader, and we're all well aware that not everyone was meant to be a manager either. The best companies are the ones that have figured out that dynamic and look for and hire the best of each.

Tom Peters says this better than I can: "Management is about arranging and telling, Leadership is about nurturing and enhancing."

LESS IS MORE

• • •

"Less is more" is a short phrase that I love. It has a lot of meaning and I have tried to follow that philosophy with many projects and business decisions I've had to make. It originated from a poem by Robert Browning called "Andrea del Sarto," written in 1855. Here is the specific section from the poem:

> Who strive—you don't know how the others strive
> To paint a little thing like that you smeared
> Carelessly passing with your robes afloat,
> Yet do much less, so much less, someone says,
> (I know his name, no matter)—so much less!
> Well, less is more, Lucrezia.

Years later, an architect and furniture designer named Ludwig Mies van der Rohe was also linked to the phrase based on his style and focus on the simplicity of style; i.e., Less is More.

In business, there are times when a lot of detail is needed, but I think, more often than not, we make things too complicated. Meetings are too long and focused, reports are eight pages instead of two, and PowerPoint presentations become long and drawn out with bullets stating the obvious. To me, "less is more" means cut to the chase, keep things simple, and make it understandable.

Frankly, 95 percent of the time when I have had to present to senior executives, they preferred the summary to the long story. "Less is More" is a great strategy and well worth trying follow.

LET PEOPLE OFF
THE HOOK

● ● ●

It seems like, in this day and age, we're ready to pounce on people who make a mistake. We'll watch some politician or celebrity make a dumb statement and then social media will light up for days attacking the person. I'm not referring to hideous behavior, as that more than warrants the negative feedback. I'm referring to verbal slips or an embarrassing incident during an interview.

The same thing happens in competitive business environments too. Someone will send out a promotional email blast with an error and the marketer will get chastised. A finance manager will miscalculate an expense item and it impacts how results are reported. Or maybe a salesperson quotes the wrong price and a customer gets an amazing deal that takes away any profit margin.

How about we recognize the mistake, discuss it, make a point of making sure it never happens again, and then let people off the hook so they can regroup and improve their ways going forward? Of course, if something unethical or illegal was done, then that's an entirely different situation, and a rescue line is most likely not warranted. If this is the second or third time that someone has made the same mistake, then instead of letting the person off the hook, you may want to guide him to new job elsewhere.

It's not dismissing glaring mistakes or burying them under the rug; it's evaluating the situation and individual with a bit of compassion. Maybe this is a time to let the person off the hook.

LINKEDIN PROFILE AND YOUR RESUME

● ● ●

When was the last time you updated your resume and LinkedIn profile? Most people haven't updated it in more than a year, and that's just foolish. Does your resume have useless words like, "detail-oriented," "team player," and "dedicated"? Is your LinkedIn profile photo one when you had a different hairstyle? Is it professional-looking or a quick selfie taken in your kitchen?

These are simple things to correct but, more often than not, we say that we'll get to it next week. However, I've found that people procrastinate so much with their resume and LinkedIn updating and then have a panic attack when someone requests them.

You're happy in your current job and don't need to update your materials, right? Suppose someone came along tomorrow and told you about a job that was absolutely amazing. Or, from a more negative perspective, but certainly realistic, what happens if your company announces major cuts or is acquired tomorrow? Will you be ready?

Pick a day, some evening, or a rainy Saturday morning and get this done. If you're still hesitating, then spend a few dollars and hire a professional to do it for you. Neglecting your resume and LinkedIn profile is doing you a real disservice but can be remedied so quickly.

LISTENING SKILLS AND THE ART OF NOT SPEAKING

● ● ●

When corporate trainers are asked what often separates the good businesspeople from weak ones, inevitably, listen-ing skills is on that list. It seems many of us spend too much time talking, not asking enough questions, and not listening.

There are literally hundreds of articles about the impor-tance of listening and it's a topic in business courses, along with leadership and management books. We all know the impor-tance of it and most of us understand how much it can set us back when we don't give full attention, yet it's still an issue for many employees. Most people can stand to improve their listening skills, whether they think so or not.

Listening is a skill that needs to be practiced. It requires you to step back for moment, shut your own mouth, forget about your response that you're ready to share with everyone, and actually place someone else's thoughts or opinions ahead of yours. It's not easy and, as I said, it requires work to master it.

How many times from your days in school or work have you encountered a soft-spoken person who doesn't speak much, but when the does, everyone stops to hear her thoughts? Conversely, how many times have we come across the individual who just doesn't stop talking and, as soon as he speaks, you are shutting them out?

Listeners are the ones who solve problems. They give their full attention to the other person speaking after they've ask a question. They focus on the conversation, they don't interrupt, and they ask follow-up questions to clarify points to ensure they've heard everything correctly. They are showing interest and, even more importantly, respect for the other person talking.

The first step is to recognize the importance of listening and then diligently practice it over a period of time. Listen, don't speak, and see if you notice the difference it makes.

LOFTY TITLES AND FANCY DEGREES—DON'T BE INTIMIDATED

● ● ●

If you've gone to college and then continued on to get an advanced degree, whether it be a master's or a PhD, you should be very proud of your accomplishment. You must have worked hard, studied long hours, and written more than just a few papers here and there. Similarly, in business when your title changes to manager, director, vice president or maybe even one at the most senior levels, you deserve a pat on the back. As you advance in your career, along with the financial impact, it is a nice feeling to have your work recognized by receiving a title that carries more weight in the organization. Your peers and colleagues will be aware of your work and accomplishments, so there won't be a need to regularly remind them.

Through the years, I have worked with some really smart people. They've gotten MBAs from great universities and some had PhDs too. Along the way, I've reported to people who were pretty high up on the organizational chart. Early in my career, I used to get intimidated by those who had advanced degrees or were very senior within the company. Over time, however, I came to realize that, in most cases, they were no different than me. They had flaws like anyone, business experiences like the rest of us, and, at times, questioned their own skills too.

For the most part, the senior leaders didn't flaunt their status levels within the company. There were a few who did become legendary for being snobs in elevators, having limos outside the building waiting for them, or nodding and not acknowledging lower-ranked people sitting in a business review. In time, I concluded their behavior was their weakness, not mine.

Then there were the other colleagues who needed to remind us where they went to college or that "they recently had a discussion on that topic in the mergers and acquisitions class in their MBA program."

Are you nodding your head as your reading this? Every company has individuals like these people, whose confidence levels are actually weak, which is why they need to remind everyone about their degrees or titles. You don't need a lofty title or a lot of letters after your name to be successful or a leader. You can be impressed with people who've achieved those levels or degrees, but don't let them intimidate you.

LOOK IN THE MIRROR. DO YOU LIKE WHAT YOU SEE?

● ● ●

Sometimes, in business, we wonder if we're doing the right thing. Maybe we question a decision we're making, since it's approaching the edge of being heavy-handed, a bit too aggressive, or maybe it's a little too close to having some ethical issue.

I've encountered situations like that every so often in my career and I have a simple exercise that quickly helps give me the proper direction. It works every time, and I've recommended it to colleagues often when I've been asked for advice on a touchy matter.

If you're unsure or are questioning your actions, remember this statement: "At the end of the day, you have to able to look at yourself in the mirror, and if you don't like what you see or what you're saying, you need to change your ways."

It's very simple, yet very powerful when you see your own eyes staring back at you in the mirror, watching your lips move, and your ears hearing what you say. It all ties back to the basics of being authentic, being credible, and having personal integrity. You can never lose sight of that.

LOOK OUT FOR YOURSELF

● ● ●

I truly believe that we should try to help others, show empathy and compassion when it's needed, and be a friend to others in both good and bad times. It is something I've tried to practice throughout my life. For the most part, I've been fortunate to have worked with people professionally and in my personal life who follow those same principles. However, there are others who are what I call "fair-weather friends."

You know who I mean, since we all have encountered them in our lives. They're all supportive and cheerful with you on sunny days, but when the tide turns and maybe your "value" to them has diminished, they vanish when you ask them for a helping hand.

We develop and build up a lot of acquaintances in our lives through work, our neighborhoods, and where we socialize. However, our list of true friends, those you can count on like family, is a smaller list than you think.

My apologies if this sounds negative but it's a subtle remember to always look out for yourself. It's another plug for never forgetting that family comes first.

LOSING A JOB—THE CYCLE OF EMOTIONS

● ● ●

Let's face it: losing a job can happen to anyone. Companies seem to be much more open to making changes to organizational structures faster than ever before. It doesn't matter whether you've been in your job two years or twenty, the focus on expense management and return on investment for your specific position is very intense. If it does happen to you, don't feel ashamed or embarrassed, since I guarantee you have friends and neighbors who have also been impacted at some point in their careers too. (Note: I'm not referring to losing your job because you did something unethical and were dismissed.)

In each of the companies I've worked for, there have been many instances when people I knew have been let go. Unfortunately, there have also been many times when I was the person who had to deliver the bad news. I've seen the reactions firsthand, heard the feedback, and witnessed a very clear cycle of emotions. Everyone goes through them in varying degrees.

Here are a few of the emotions that people feel.

- Depending on the company and the circumstances, anger is very common.
- There's a questioning of, "Why me?"
- You feel like you're just a number and not a loyal employee.

- Varying levels of sadness, ranging from mild to hysterical crying.
- Anger needs to be listed again, because some people can't put what happened behind them and move on.
- There is a panic phase of not knowing what you're going to do next.
- You would be surprised at how many times people say they feel relieved. The waiting for "it" to happen was torturous, so being let go at least ends the "uncertainty."
- I've seen people who take it as a reflection of their worth and drift into a state approaching depression. You need to watch for this if you know someone like this.
- Resolve and acceptance are what some people feel. "Okay, it's over. I'll take my severance and move on."

LOYALTY TO
FRIENDS AND YOUR
COMPANY

● ● ●

It can be can similar to the recovery process from the loss of a loved one. Your mind spins with thoughts and you need to recognize that the cycle of emotions is a part of the healing process.

In a number of the entries in this book, I've written about the importance of looking out for yourself and that your family always comes first. That is something I truly believe in and those priorities are critical to understand.

There is also something to be said about loyalty to the people who've hired you, mentored you, and for the company where you're working. There are probably varying levels of loyalty, depending on the relationships you've had and the support you've received. I'm sure you've experienced situations where you would be right there, arm-in-arm, so to speak, with certain managers you've had. Conversely, I'm sure for, some, the loyalty ends at the end of the work day.

I believe in loyalty and you should make it factor with some of your decision-making, but it does have its limits. There have been more than a few occasions when I've spoken to a friend or work colleague who I think have taken loyalty too far. The person expressed some guilt about looking for a new job or interviewing at a different company because he felt some loyalty to his hiring manager or his employer. "They've been so good to me," or, "I'm loyal to my company that hired me right out of college and gave me this chance."

Thoughts like that should be respected and even admired, but you need some refocus and reminding about what your priorities should be. Loyalty to friends, your manager, and your company carry a fair amount of significance sometimes, but you and your family should always be first on that list.

MEETINGS

• • •

The word "Meetings" is guaranteed to get a reaction from everyone. It's on everyone's list of things that we don't like about our jobs. We complain that there are too many of them, they're too long, or even a complete waste of time. For as long as I can recall, the mere mention of "meetings" is enough to get businesspeople riled up.

There are so many articles with tips on how not to let meetings fill up your entire calendar. Yet I bet your planner is currently filled with dozens of meetings. Some are the standing, ongoing various weekly meeting with peers, the monthly check-in with your manager, and a few are ones you own that have been in place for more than a year.

I think it's worth considering taking an online course about improving meetings you attend or manage. In fact, I think this type of training should be required for employees at all levels of a corporation. Managing a meeting, setting an agenda, and how you behave in meetings can easily separate the professional from the amateur. I'm not saying this lightly; I believe careers can be impacted positively and negatively based on how you "handle" meetings.

Here are seven pet peeves that I have about meetings.

- ✐ Attending a Meeting Unprepared
    - ○ This is a surefire way to annoy more than just a few people: going to a meeting when you haven't

read the advance material beforehand and aren't ready to participate. You're wasting your time and other attendees' time by even showing up. What is amazing is how many times I've heard people say, "I didn't have time to download and read any of the prep work. Sorry." Really?

- ⟲ Showing up Late or Forgetting about It
  - o I'm a real old grouch about this one, but if the meeting starts at 10:00, don't stroll in at 10:08. It means you've disrupted the meeting that's already underway and then you need to get a quick summary of what's been discussed. How can you just forget? Every office has that person who says, "Oh I'm really sorry, but I got wrapped up in another project and totally forgot about your meeting." That doesn't fly for me.

- ⟲ Talking Too Much
  - o There's always someone who feels he has to say something in every meeting and then takes it to the next level and pontificates. This is also a reflection on the meeting host, who should be cutting off the garrulous person.

- ⟲ Running the Meeting Without Having a Clear Objective or Agenda
  - o If you schedule a meeting and invite people to prepare and attend, you should have a clear objective for the meeting and a well-defined agenda. Sending out materials the day of the meeting and handing out an agenda still warm from the copy machine is not the way to do it.

⌀ Unable to Read Your Audience

    o   Being able to read your audience is an important skill that you must learn if you want your career to develop. It's especially important if you're running a meeting. Can you see which attendees are still engaged or whether people are fidgeting or half asleep? You also need to keep the discussion orderly to make certain people aren't having side conversations or speaking over each other. If you're unable to read your audience, you're wasting people's time.

⌀ Mobile Phone and Tablet Use

    o   Okay, I'm an old grouch with this too. Yes, I realize that people are taking notes and checking materials distributed online, but don't tell me you're multi-tasking. You have to look up and listen to people speaking. I think it's insulting to see a room of heads lowered like everyone is praying. This is even worse when you have a guest speaker, client, or supplier making a presentation.

⌀ The One-hour Mandatory Meeting for Every Employee

    o   For several years, there is a regularly scheduled meeting with almost every employee. Over time, attendance has grown, and the agenda has become a political football of who gets to add items. And, with so many employees working in remote locations, you lose time when the conference number doesn't work, or someone forgets to mute the line and you mute and you hear Muzak for ten minutes. Every few months, you should re-evaluate these regular-set meetings to see if they're still worth holding.

You could probably add a few more pet peeves of your own. The bottom line: how you handle meetings can make or break your career. If you have any concerns about your approach in meetings, I encourage you to take a course on the skills of running a successful meeting.

MENTAL HEALTH DAYS

● ● ●

We can have the greatest job imaginable, but there are still times when we may feel overwhelmed, frustrated, angry, stressed, or totally exhausted. There's nothing uncommon about these feelings, but you don't need to be a doctor to realize that if those situations are occurring more frequently or are now daily issues, then you need to do something now!

Our health is often impacted by what happens at work. We've all experienced some tossing and turning in bed when we think about some project and then we wake up exhausted. Have you ever experienced anxiety when you're called into a meeting with your manager that you suspect may be confrontational?

These aren't healthy situations and you should listen to what your body is telling you. See a doctor if you have symptoms of an illness and get assistance to remedy those issues. Don't be embarrassed or worried about seeing someone for psychological issues. You should never be shy about seeking professional help.

You may be familiar with the phrase, "Take a mental health day." I'm a big believer in them and, over the years, I've gotten some funny looks from people when I say that, every so often, it's a smart idea to take one. We all need to just escape sometimes and get away from work. I think it makes our minds clearer and we just feel better. You've got sick days or personal days available, so go use one every so often. Get a massage, go see a movie, head off to the mall, or just stay home and read a book. Believe me, there's nothing wrong with taking mental health days occasionally and your company will survive without you for a day. Try it out. Put one of those days in your calendar right now.

MODEL THE WAY

• • •

There's a great book written by James Kouzes and Barry Posner called, *The Leadership Challenge*. The authors have been instrumental in training thousands of businesspeople through the years. In the book, and as a part of the training, you learn about the "five practices of exemplary leadership."

It starts with "Model the Way," and in their words, "Leaders establish principles concerning the way people (constituents, peers, colleagues, and customers alike) should be treated and the way goals should be pursued. They create standards of excellence and then set an example for others to follow."

That seems so logical, so simple, and so powerful. As leaders, we all lead by example and hopefully the standards you're setting are of the highest quality. I think when you "model the way," you can distinguish yourself as an exemplary leader and your reward will be seeing those who report to you and work with you achieving higher levels of success. They will perform to the best of their ability and will feel engaged and enjoy their work.

What a great objective for all us to improve our leadership skills to such a level that we are truly able to "Model the Way."

MORALE IN
BUSINESS AND ITS
IMPACT ON YOU

● ● ●

Have you ever woken up on a Monday morning and really dreaded going to work? I think we've all been there and it's pretty common to experience times in our jobs when we wished we were somewhere else. This could be the result of various issues ranging from a boring job to a micromanaging boss. It also could be because the atmosphere and morale are so poor at your employer that it can be downright depressing.

Bad morale in a company can do extreme damage if you let it fester or steps aren't taken to try and improve it. People feel unmotivated, work suffers across the board, and employees end up leaving. Usually the best people, the ones the company can ill afford to lose, are those who head to the exits first for another job elsewhere.

Energy gets sucked out of an organization because of bad morale. It is the seed that triggers gossip and secret conversations that, in turn, hinders overall performance. It can get even worse if management fails to recognize it and doesn't communicate to everyone that the issues will be listened to and addressed. When this happens, the work environment becomes "us" vs. "them."

When bad morale reaches the point of crippling a department or the entire company, the culture can be damaged almost irreparably. Low or bad morale takes upbeat and optimistic people and turns them into mediocre coworkers.

You need to spot situations like this quickly and not let them drag you down. If you can be the one to help improve the atmosphere, then you are a leader and will be respected. If you sense that the morale is approaching dangerous levels, that's your signal to move on quickly to a better situation.

MULTITASKING

• • •

Some people act very confident and are so sure of themselves when say that they're good at multitasking. Their voice is firm, they give you a focused stare and even straighten up a bit as they explain that they're more skilled than anyone else. I don't agree, and I even think your work suffers because of it. In some cases, I think it's a sign of disrespect when others see you attempting it.

I'm not referring to those of us who multitask when preparing a dinner while, at the same time, are watching the evening news off in the distance or maybe chatting on the telephone. I even give a lot of leeway if you're on a long conference call, the phone is on mute, and you take some time to delete a few emails or respond with some quick replies.

What bothers me are the people who you can hear typing continuously when you're on the phone with them. They're not taking notes; they're doing email correspondence while you're attempting to make a point or provide them with information. The worst culprits are the ones who blatantly multitask when you're in a group meeting. They sit there with their tablet or mobile phone typing or reading while someone else is speaking. You may be able to do several tasks simultaneously, but when you're in a meeting, you've now made a public statement that the person talking doesn't deserve your full attention. It's a negative refection on you that people remember more than you make think.

In a business setting, focus on one thing at a time, do it properly, and save multitasking for those occasions when you're alone.

NEGATIVE ATTITUDE

• • •

Thankfully, for most of my life, I have been an optimist. I try see to the positive side of things while, at the same time, being realistic. Of course, there have been many times when my attitude has been poor, my mood gloomy, and I've felt more than a bit negative. I believe we all go through stages of highs and lows. The trick is to try and make sure our highs don't get too out-of-control and our lows don't drag us into long stretches of dark days.

The fact is we're all different and some of us are just more positive than others. There's nothing wrong with people balancing that out with a dose of reality every so often. In fact, I don't mind when someone I work with points out things than can go wrong in a semi- negative way. That frank honesty can sometimes be annoying, but it can flag a potential issue before it becomes a bigger problem.

However, sometimes negative people can be a real dead-weight when you're trying to get something accomplished. They'll make statements like, "That won't work," or, "It will cost too much," or, "We don't have a chance to win." They're the folks who insist it will rain tomorrow when it's sunny out today. I much prefer having the ratio of people I know and spend time with heavily skewed to those who have a positive attitude.

Note: If you have more than your fair share of negative days, dark days, or you're finding that they are increasing and maybe even becoming more of the norm, you should seek professional guidance. The line crossing into depression from ordinary feeling-a-little-low is tough to recognize but if you sense that you're negative more often, seek expert help. It's the smart thing that you must do before negativity spirals into something potentially worse.

NETWORKING IS SO IMPORTANT

• • •

When I meet with people in the course of my coaching work, there is one subject that is guaranteed to generate a reaction. This is true for those people who may be looking to improve their business skills and for those who are searching for a job. In both situations, I always discuss the importance of networking and my clients inevitably groan or roll their eyes. For whatever reason, people see networking as some sort of painful ordeal and view "having to connect" with people a struggle.

I've spent the majority of my career in sales, and when I bring up cold-calling in training sessions, I'll a get similar reaction. Networking and cold-calling have similarities. I think it comes down to a fear of the unknown, being in uncomfortable situations, or getting a negative response or even rejection.

With networking, we're concerned about intruding; we may feel shy about meeting new people or we're not sure about what to say when we do connect. You may not be totally comfortable with networking, but it is an important skill to learn if you want cultivate new career opportunities and to be successful in any field. You might as well stop complaining and just accept the fact that you need to learn to network and do more of it.

My recommendation is that you view networking as an investment in yourself. It will enable you to not just meet new people but to learn new ideas, expose yourself to different concepts, and expand your thinking outside of the smaller safe zone you're in now.

You have to take the first step. Start with reaching out to someone new whom you may know from business, an acquaintance you met a conference, or someone from a class or seminar you're taking. Start with just one person and you'll see that it is not as difficult as you might think. Just start networking!

NETWORKING WITH LINKEDIN

● ● ●

Using LinkedIn for meeting new people is an easy and painless way to network. You've got two hundred, three hundred, five hundred, or maybe thousands of connections already. Scroll through your connections and write down a list—five or twenty—of people with whom you want to reach out again.

Don't select some random person you accepted an invite from following a conference two years ago. Choose people such as those with whom you worked in the past or had some other business connection in common. Do a friendly check-in to see how business is or how the individual is doing at her new employer. You might not hear back quickly from each person, but I promise you will get replies from a few, and that starts the process.

The other option, which is even less stressful, is to participate in the commentary within the daily posts and articles on LinkedIn. Your thinking is outdated if you're assuming LinkedIn is just for recruiting. I read articles and posts each day and I add my own feedback when I feel I can contribute something constructive to the conversation. Offer an opinion or pass along some ideas and respond directly to people in your replies. You'll be surprised at the number of new people you will meet this way. More importantly, I guarantee you will learn some new concepts and ways of doing your work smarter and more successfully.

NEVER BE
"THAT" PERSON

● ● ●

At every gathering of family or friends, there's the point when someone will say loudly with a smile on his face, "Do you remember that one time when so-and-so did that crazy thing?" Or, "Do you remember that time freshman year when he or she fell asleep during the lecture in the front row?" It could be ten, fifteen, even twenty years ago, but people have amazing memories of embarrassing moments when someone's done something silly or, perhaps, a bit over the edge. With family and with friends, all this ribbing is done in fun.

In business, though, you don't want to be remembered for the sophomoric behavior of years ago. It's best to be mindful of your behavior, especially in certain professional settings. Here are some examples of what to avoid: You don't want to be the person who talks too much during meetings or the person remembered for having had one too many cocktails at the corporate function.

Along those lines, you can add gossip and too much information to the list of red flags of the type person you don't want to be known as. The gossipers are also probably a part of that same group of our lovely colleagues who tell you everything going on in their lives, from family squabbles to the status of some elective surgery they've had. To be honest, I like hearing stories about people's children and family travels, but there does come a point when people just share too much information.

How do you know if you are one those people? Well, you need to be aware of your surroundings, assess the feel of a meeting room, watch the body language from those sitting there, and the eye contact you are getting from people with whom you're communicating. As businesspeople, assessing the situation and how we are perceived is critically important. If people are rolling their eyes, fidgeting a lot, or don't respond to your statements at all, then you are getting a clear message. Self-evaluation, recognizing signs whcrc you need to improve, and then taking remedial action to alter your behavior and image is important.

NEVER BLAME OTHERS

• • •

There are some things that people do that create such a poor image of themselves and that can often tarnish their reputations for a long time. One of the big "Don'ts" that annoys everyone is the person who blames everyone else for a situation they may be in. You can even see it in the facial expression of others who listen, and you know that they find the blaming to be so arrogant. It makes you want to say that to that person, "Oh come on. Grow up, will you?"

Interestingly, you'll see this happen with individuals at all levels within a company. However, it can be especially offensive if the individual is in a leadership role or senior executive position. However, I think we all can give examples of people who really should know better, but whine about the situation they're in.

People who blame others are never respected, even if they may actually be right. They feel the world is against them, someone else is always at fault, they often have a sour demeanor, and they're afraid to take ownership. Who wants to be around people like that? I sure don't.

Leaders are formed and developed at all levels within an organization. If some bad fate comes your way, don't look to divert the blame to someone else. Accept what's happened, move forward, and look for ways to remedy the issue quickly. This style will be clearly recognized by others and you will gain respect, admiration, and been seen as a leader.

NEVER DISCUSS RELIGION AND POLITICS—OR AT LEAST BE CAREFUL

● ● ●

In this era where social media is so accessible, over-sharing our beliefs and opinions is something I think you need to be careful doing. What we say and post online, especially in business settings, can be risky. Our colleagues, connections, and our customers come from many backgrounds, religions, political, and social beliefs.

Frankly, good discussions can take place when people of differing views meet and analyze them in an open and honest way. We learn new concepts, and, in some cases, our thinking may be altered or refined. That's healthy and important for us as individuals and as a society.

However, you know that in our world today it seems like we're split 50-50 on any subject. This book is about business situations and that's why say, more often than not, I don't want to hear your opinions on politics, religion, or social matters. There's a right time and place. At the start of a meeting about marketing plans, I'd prefer to not have someone bring up yesterday's controversial tweet by a conservative or a liberal.

You may not agree with me, but at least be mindful and prudent.

NEVER DISCUSS SEX
AND HEALTH

● ● ●

We all know the phrase "TMI," meaning "too much information." Why do certain people feel the need to divulge personal information in public settings? Every office has a few of these people and they create cringe-worthy moments when they let us know about some personal matters. Of course, there's a difference if you're talking to your close friend in a private spot and you both feel comfortable exchanging details of things. I'm referring to more public situations.

Let's start with health. Mentioning that you're going to the doctor for a check-up is one thing, but giving details about a specific exam is a bit over-the-top. I once sat in a meeting when a colleague explained in gory detail exactly how he felt during a procedure. No one wanted to know, and no one wanted to listen since it's nobody's business.

A number of years ago, I arrived into a conference room early for a meeting, and a few others were there chatting about their various activities over the weekend. At one point, someone started talking about some very intimate details while at a spa with her partner. From across the conference room table, I tried at first to ignore it, but after a minute I said, "You're kidding, right?" Of course, the person looked at me like I was the odd one.

There's a right time and a wrong time to talk about private matters involving your health and sexual activity. You should know not to cross that barrier and, if you don't, reread this entry.

NEVER DISPARAGE
YOUR COMPETITION

● ● ●

The pressure to grow our businesses and increase profitability is so intense. We're faced with challenges in the marketplace, ever-changing customer interests, and competitors who are getting stronger and nimbler. This stress can cause some people to consider tactics that they normally wouldn't use. Some businesspeople break an ethical code and go down a path disparaging the competition. This strategy is never successful and making derogatory comments or posting negative statements about other companies or individuals can only backfire in the long run.

A number of years ago, I had business contact call me up to say that a competitor was making disparaging remarks about me. I was more than annoyed at the person making those statements, but it was his reputation and respect that was tarnished in my business contact's eyes for being so unprofessional. The competitor not only lost the business, but a lot more.

Competition is a part of business. I like to think that it makes us all more effective when we face the best from another company. Let your hard work, preparation, planning, and presentation drive your process. Then, most importantly, let your product or service, along with your reputation and credibility, allow you to beat the competition.

NEVER GIVE UP

• • •

This is a saying that is often the basis for one of those motivational posters you'll see advertised. There's a photo of a person climbing up a rocky mountainside looking as if he is about to fall, and underneath it, in bold type, it says, "Never Give Up." I don't know about you, but if I'm clinging to edge of a cliff, I'm sure going to be hollering for some help.

What I'm referring to here aligns more with believing in yourself and not giving in to disappointment or admitting failure too soon. There are times when we face some pretty big obstacles and the easy way out may seem to be accepting defeat or just assuming that the competition is better than us. It feels lousy, we shrug our shoulders, and then we say that maybe it just wasn't meant to be. After all of that hard work, planning, and preparation we walk away waving the white flag of surrender.

Instead, in these situations, step back for minute and remember that you're good at what at you do, but maybe this time your efforts so far have fallen short. My advice is to give it another shot, be persistent, and be confident in your abilities. Sometimes the extra attempt or last additional push will enable you to achieve the goal you want and the success you deserve to achieve.

NEVER HOLD A
GRUDGE

● ● ●

This is one of those things that's easier said than done. We've been hearing this advice probably since elementary school. The fact is it just doesn't make sense to hold a grudge. Somebody may say something negative about us, let us down, or were just plain mean and it has upset and angered us. We pace a bit, we think about it, and we may even lose some sleep thinking of ways to get back at the culprit. Then a friend, family member, a mentor, or some other colleague will say to us, "Oh, just move on. Don't hold a grudge. You're better than that." Does this ring a bell?

Holding a grudge really is a waste of time. What's done is done and you can't go back to the way things were before whatever happened. Through the years, I've gotten better at this, but I'd be lying if I said it was easier. There is another saying that links closely to situations like this—"Forgive and Forget."

I'm all for that and it means that you don't let a grudge be an anchor to slow you down. You may be 100 percent right, but after a certain amount of time, holding a grudge actually makes you look petty and weak. I'll spin the advice a bit differently. Learn from what has happened to you. Express your displeasure from what wrong may have occurred. But take the high road and move on. You'll feel better for moving on and respected for doing so. You forgive, maybe not forget totally, but your positive actions will make you shine over those of the offending person.

NON-DISCLOSURE AGREEMENTS

● ● ●

Non-disclosure agreements, NDAs, are fairly common in business settings when meeting with clients, customers, or other companies. Information may be discussed that one party wants to ensure doesn't get discussed outside of a restricted group of people. In these situations, you'll hear the person running the meeting say, "I need you to sign an NDA before we proceed. Okay?" People nod their heads, say, "Yes, of course," signatures are given, and the proceedings move on.

What you need to realize is that signing an NDA isn't just a more formal way of your connection expressing a desire to keep something confidential. It is a legal agreement and, if you break that trust, you will lose more than your credibility—you could get in real trouble.

Not sure whether to sign an NDA or not? Then don't sign it. In fact, a good lesson is never sign anything without checking with you company's legal representative first. Did you hear what I just said? Never sign anything unless it is reviewed first by someone with legal expertise who understands agreements and contracts. That includes NDAs.

OFFICE ROMANCE

• • •

If you work with people eight to ten hours day, week in and week out, month after month, we would be naïve to think that casual business relationships sometimes don't develop into something a bit more. There has been extensive advice about appropriate behavior and what to do and not do. But it's an important subject, so I am going to give some brief advice, based on my personal experience as well as my time as a manger. I've been married for more than three decades to woman I met when we worked at the same company. She was in advertising, I was in sales, there was a party, and the rest is history. We decided that being with the same company, in the same building, even in different departments and business units would not be good for us. My wife left the company to work somewhere else; for us it was a wise decision. That said, I know many people who are married or have partners who work at the same offices together and they make it work. I don't know how they do it, but they do. Many companies have policies prohibiting couples from working in the same business units and I think that is a wise policy. So, what happens when we look at office romance from a different perspective? You're married or with a significant other. Let's go back to my statement that, "If you work with people eight to ten hours day, week in and week out, month after month, we would be naïve to think that casual business relationships sometimes don't develop into something a bit more." It's pretty common and I'm not judging, but if you think nobody knows, believe me, everybody knows. Enough said.

PARTICIPATE AND
RAISE YOUR HAND

• • •

Much like avoiding public speaking, we often shy away from participating in group meetings or training sessions for fear of saying something wrong, not wanting to appear ignorant, or because we're intimidated by others in the room. Some people really enjoy joining committees or a task force. They're the exact opposite of the ones who are reluctant as they feel that they'll miss out on something if they don't sign up.

This entry is about employees who don't participate in anything at all. The work is nine to five, you do your job, and you go home. There's nothing wrong with that, but I think you're letting some potentially fun activities or learning opportunities pass you by. Do you need to join every special interest club at the office, be a member of the focus group team, or volunteer three nights a week at the local charity? No, of course not.

However, don't let everything slip by you. Start with just one opportunity that comes your way. Sign up for it, make a call, or raise your hand to say yes. I think you'll be glad you did.

PERCEPTIONS WE HAVE OF PEOPLE— ARE THEY RIGHT OR WRONG?

● ● ●

Over the course of my career, I have had the opportunity to meet people from many different backgrounds and professions. From accountants, salespeople, and lawyers to programmers, nurses, and recent college graduates, I have enjoyed the diversity of people I have met and learning more about the jobs they have held. They speak with pride of the financial analyses they may be doing, the sales they have made, enthusiasm for a project completed, or the excitement to enter the "real" world after four years of college. It is all genuine and authentic.

Interestingly, without me asking, often people will make a comment about some perception or stereotype that people have about their occupation. I have had an advertising executive tell me that people think his world is like the TV show *Mad Men*. An accountant expressed her dismay that everyone in her profession is perceived to be a bean-counter. A bond salesman said he gets frustrated because his friends joke that he must be like some of those hard-sell sales guys we have all seen in the movies.

Where do these stereotypes come from? Often, it could be just misconceptions of what jobs entail. For example, those who are accountants or in advertising are often unfairly characterized. The other possibility could be what someone told me recently, saying that 2 percent of the people in every profession exhibit odd or poor behavior. Sadly, they do improper things and it impacts everyone. My friend is probably right about that percentage, but we must be more open and push aside those incorrect views and focus on the other 98 percent.

I am far from qualified to explore into the sociological and psychological aspects of why we stereotype or generalize about people. However, we do characterize certain jobs and professions with incorrect assumptions and end up unfairly criticizing an entire group of people.

I must confess, through the years, I have gotten a bit annoyed and even frustrated when people look at me and make references to the sales profession. That 98 percent figure I noted earlier is spot-on since we are the ones who don't use "in-your-face tactics" or sell you something you don't need or want.

Among the cornerstones that I believe are important for us to follow to overcome the misinterpretation we have of certain professions: education, asking questions, listening, being open, showing true empathy, and communication. Each of those are so important and we need to do more of them.

Therefore, think twice when someone makes a statement about a lawyer, a reporter, a police officer, stockbroker, or anyone in any profession.

PERSONAL GOALS ARE IMPORTANT TO HAVE

● ● ●

For every employer we have, we'll be asked to prepare, update, and monitor a list of objectives that we'll be required to complete. We'll get evaluated on these tasks and our success or disappointment in completing them will impact our compensation. In addition to objectives, some managers will also assign some goals for you to achieve. When most people hear the words "objectives" and "goal-setting" with regard to business, they're not happy because they assume there will be lots of work that will be tracked and possibly lead to a negative review.

However, in our personal lives, I think we should set goals and we should view them in a very positive way. Your goals need to be attainable and about achieving something. For example, you might be asking yourself where you want to be in a few years or how you want to spend free time.

You can have as many goals as you want, but I'd recommend a short list of no more than five or six. Maybe you have a goal of taking some classes this year. You have a goal of saving a few extra dollars for vacation. Whatever you set as a goal, try to work toward it this year. Actually, write your goals down somewhere where you can see them when you're working. Seeing the goals on paper or on your computer should motivate you, especially if they're things that make you happy. They provide a great counterbalance to your lists of work obligations and will help you prioritize the importance of your personal life.

PERSONAL MASTERING OF THE BASICS—YOUR WILL AND LIVING WILL

● ● ●

One of my mantras has always been "Planning and preparation." I firmly believe that these steps are essential in helping us become successful in business. Proper planning and thorough preparation also free us up to do other things. (This is a book about business skills, but I have included a few items outside of work that I feel are important and, in many ways, impact our professional life too.)

No one wants to talk about serious illnesses or the fact that someday we won't be around anymore. They're not pleasant subjects, but the reality is that we do get sick and, at some point, we will die. For all our sakes, I hope these things happen many years from now.

Do you have a will? You need to have one and, if you don't, you should schedule a meeting with a lawyer this week. Yes, there are online templates you can use but this is too important a matter not to have it drafted by a professional. When you meet with an attorney, he or she will probably ask whether you also want a living will. This document specifies your wishes regarding medical treatment should you be unable to express your desires if you are seriously ill. You should also discuss having a Power of Attorney. This gives authority to someone else to handle your financial and legal affairs should you be unable to do so.

While I'm discussing these "happy" subjects, are your financial records accessible should you get ill? How about your desires, should you die? Is there some record of how you want that handled? A service? Cemetery? You know what I mean.

Do these things now when you're healthy. Talk with your spouse, your partner, or designated relative and say you want to have these matters taken care of now. Is it uncomfortable to bring up? Of course, it is, which is why most people say, "Oh I don't want to talk about that now." Then, when something does happen, your family or friends have to try and determine what's in your best interests or guess your desires.

How to start the conversation? Blame me and just say, "I read this in a book and it is good advice. Let's get it out of the way."

PHYSICAL HEALTH—
ANNUAL EXAMS

● ● ●

This is a book about mastering business skills and I'm including something about your health? Yes, because our health, along with that of our colleagues, has an enormous impact on our work. This isn't an entry about the issue of healthcare costs either. Quite simply, I'm stressing the importance of taking care of yourself and having an annual physical exam. Some people always see their doctor once a year for their physical, the dentist two to three times annually for a cleaning, and also get their eyes examined every twelve months. But many other people haven't seen any type of doctor in years. There are too many serious illnesses that can be detected early and treated if a consistent schedule of visits to the doctor are maintained. There's no rational excuse for not going to doctor.

If your check-up history is a bit spotty, you can fix that starting tomorrow. Make the appointments with your internist, dentist, and optometrist; make them an annual habit, and you'll be better off.

PRIORITIZE AND FOCUS ON WHAT IS IMPORTANT

● ● ●

There are times when our workload can seem over-whelming. We'll have reports to complete, task force meetings to attend, emails that seem to multiply in front our eyes, last-minute requests from our manager, and oh, yes, the responsibilities that are a part of our job descriptions. That takes up our work life and then we have our obligations outside of work too. Does this sound familiar?

This scenario is something I've experienced many times in my career and it comes up regularly with virtually every business professional. You have that feeling of someone trying bail water out of a boat but you're only using a small cup. The faster you pour water out, the more comes in and you begin to feel helpless. For some people, this can lead to unhealthy conditions such as high blood pressure, anxiety, or stress-related illnesses.

As I explained in the entries on Managing Your Time and Being Organized, there are ways to reduce the stress from work obligations. However, prioritizing and focusing on what is really important is a critical skill.

Some people are able to handle many things at the same time and juggle multiple tasks. However, I think for most of us, doing so can become a real challenge, especially if it's over a long period of time. Every so often, it's worth stepping back to evaluate or remind ourselves what really matters in our life. I believe family, close friends, and health comes first. Some may feel their religion comes first and then family. However, whether family or religion, our business dealings shouldn't compete with those first two.

Then it comes down to what is really driving your business for success and profitability. Write down everything you're doing and everything that you're supposed to accomplish. Each of your tasks can't be an "A" priority, so you're going to have to assign and weight each one differently. You need to prioritize and what may have been important last year might be not as critical this year. Each of us needs to be reminded regularly to prioritize and focus on what truly matters to drive happiness and success.

PRIORITIZE YOUR GREATEST OPPORTUNITIES

● ● ●

In business, not everything can be a priority, although we have all probably worked with a manager who would never prioritize anything. They bark out commands and requests as if everything was urgent and needed to be accomplished immediately.

Quite simply, you have to focus on the opportunities that are driving the business. Yes, a group meeting to review packaging for a new product is important, but is it as critical as the launch of a new CRM for the organization that you've waited years to purchase?

If you have ten opportunities, you need to understand that you can't successfully work on all of them and complete them at the same time. Do you know what your number one priority is at all times? This ties in to another entry in this book, "What's the First Thing You're Going to Do on a Monday Morning?" Too often, we treat all opportunities equally and that's putting us at a disadvantage. Prioritizing and committing our energy to the opportunities that can have the greatest impact is what successful individuals, teams, and companies do as a standard practice.

QUARTERLY REPORTS

• • •

Publicly traded companies are required by the Securities and Exchange Commission (SEC) to file reports every three months noting their revenue, expenses, profits, and cash flow. These quarterly reports are then accompanied by commentary by senior management of the company. They reference what's worked well, pointing out successes and smart decisions made. Clarification is also provided for disappointing news by referencing unstable market conditions, foreign currency fluctuations, one-time expense hits, or seasonal timing of revenue received.

Even if you're not a CEO or CFO, you should understand the importance of quarterly reports. If you're working for any larger corporation, chances are you'll end up having to write quarterly reports. It's actually not a bad idea to reflect on the prior three months, do a post-mortem of successes and failures, and then have some historical knowledge available for the future.

Although I've saved my quarterly reports, I don't think I ever reread one. A friend of mine works at a pharmaceutical company and his description of quarterly reports is probably common for most us. The CEO has to report on the business every three months and he or she knows the top line details but also wants some additional information. A note goes out asking for a few bullet points of information from the SVPs, who then pass the message to the VPs. It then goes to Directors and Department Heads who ask their teams for quarterly reports two days after the close of the quarter. A few bullet points become two five-page reports and hours are lost preparing a document that no one really refers to ever again.

That explanation may be a bit extreme, but it's hardly far-fetched. If you are required to write a quarterly report, you need to have a plan for getting it done, hitting the key points, and submitting it as quickly as possible so you can get back to your real job. I used to see colleagues in other departments spend hours on quarterly updates and fret over the process. A crazy, bureaucratic task that's embedded in some companies? Yes, so tackle it quickly and move it on.

READ YOUR
AUDIENCE

● ● ●

Have you ever been in a meeting or sat through a presentation and when you looked around the room you could tell that a third of the people were daydreaming, a third were checking their mobile devices, and the balance had totally checked out? The presenter was so focused on the statements that he wanted to make that he had completely lost touch with the audience. That could be a real problem if you want to advance in your career, because being able to sense the mood of people, understand what triggers their interest, and get them to follow you also involves being able to read them.

We often think of this as it pertains to a group presentation, but it holds true for a small group meeting and even a one-on-one session with a colleague in the cafeteria. You need to watch for signs from people's body language. Are they twitching, fidgeting, and clearly becoming impatient? Or are they asking questions and taking notes? Are their eyes glassy and seemingly staring right through you? These are easy-to-spot mannerisms, but you have to be aware and try to spot them.

Some presenters just don't get it or just don't understand and you'll soon hear them ridiculed behind their back. Meanwhile, the speakers who are engaged, listening, assessing the room, and adjusting their points, if need be, are the ones who are respected and admired.

I think the skill of being able to read your audience shows that you don't put yourself ahead of others. You care and you show interest in people at all levels within your organization. Focus on this, practice it, look to continually improve this ability, and I believe you will be a businessperson destined for more leadership roles. That's how important a skill I believe it is.

REMEMBERING
PEOPLE'S NAMES
MEANS SO MUCH

● ● ●

Listening skills are critically important in both business and in our personal lives. Good listeners give their full attention to the other person speaking after the individual asks a question. They focus on the conversation, they don't interrupt, and they ask follow-up questions to clarify points to ensure they've heard everything correctly. They are showing interest and, even more importantly, respect for the other person talking.

Closely tied to listening and the aspect of respect is remembering names and other details about people we meet. How many times have you met someone who says, "I'm awful with names"? The fact is we all have those moments where our minds go blank and, for the life of us, we just can't remember someone's name. However, we've all run across people who we have been introduced to multiple times and they draw a blank when they look at us. To me, that's a signal that they just don't care.

When someone introduces himself to you, it's important to actually listen and respond back with his name. It's no guarantee that you'll remember the next time you see the person, but it should at least give you a fighting chance. Remembering someone's name is a sign of respect and people appreciate that you've taken care to do so. It is especially important as a businessperson and will impact everyone you meet from the support staff, mid-level manager, or executive. Listening closely, paying attention, and remembering people's names is more than just a nice skill set; it's a critical step in being a successful business professional. As my first manager once told me, never pass up the opportunity to keep your mouth closed and your ears open.

REWARD THOSE YOU
WORK WITH

● ● ●

How many of you have a folder in your desk drawer or a folder on your computer that contains a letter or email from a manager, coworker, or customer that said something nice about you? They may have complimented you on some extra work you did, a project that was successful, or the product or service you provided them was really terrific. I hope you have had that experience and, if you have, I bet some of that correspondence may be five, ten, or more years old. I actually have a note from my first manager that he wrote to me more than thirty years ago that said I was doing a really good job in my new role as a field representative. Wow, did that make me feel good and want to do even better going forward so I could continue to make him feel happy about my work.

I've been lucky in my career to have worked with some terrific managers who motivated me to perform even better by providing me with positive reinforcement along with constructive criticism along the way. However, I did have a few managers from whom I never heard anything good. They thought that if I achieved my sales targets, opened up some new business, and did my reports on time then I was just doing my job.

The lesson is: Create a culture and environment where people support each other, view success as a team, and recognize positive achievements. You'd be surprised how much people can feed off that energy to become even better and achieve even more.

Rewarding, supporting, and recognizing those we work with is an important motivator and the sign of a strong individual or leader whether you're in sales or not. A simple note, a telephone call, or a personal visit to an individual can make such a difference in enhancing the motivation of that person. It will also make you feel good. So, give it try and I bet you'll feel the rewards too.

RUMORS, GOSSIP, AND SPECULATION

● ● ●

It may seem like gossip is just harmless chatter, but I think it can be one of more toxic things that can occur in a business environment. Gossip is one the biggest time-wasters there is and can often create undo stress in your company or harm people unfairly with incorrect or even hurtful misstatements.

It often rears its ugly head during times of change or uncertainty in a company. Someone tells a colleague that, "They heard there may be expense cuts," or, "Staff reductions are bound to happen in this department." Then, you before you know it, this gossip has now become gospel in certain circles. Then there is always the case of the word on the street about acquisitions or senior management changes. Once again, everyone gets wound up expressing opinions, making more false statements, and just adding fuel to the fire.

There is a game that is played by kids and sometimes even adults. You whisper a short statement into the first person's ear and that person then whispers it to the next person. This continues around the room until everyone has heard the story and the last person tells everyone out loud. You can guarantee that the subject and content has changed. It's been embellished or altered to some degree. That's what happens to gossip too. Each day it grows more like a weed.

When I would hear statements about pending changes, big announcements, and then see people consumed with trying to decipher it all, it bothered me so much. I would put an end to it by saying that unless you've heard it from the CEO, the head of Human Resources, or there's been an official company press release, then everything you are hearing is gossip.

Never be a source or a spreader of gossip. Having the reputation of being a gossiper is tough to change. It makes you look unprofessional and impacts your credibility as a respected colleague or leader.

SAY "HELLO"

● ● ●

I know. I know. I'm sounding like an old grouch with this one, but it is one of those things that has always been a thorn in my side.

It used to irk me to no end when I would walk down the hallway in the office, I'd say, "Hi" to someone and the response would be a nod or a mumble. I'd continue to walk and then raise my hands up high wondering what the heck is wrong with that person. There were a few people with whom I would just get ready to raise my hands in frustration as soon as I saw them.

I get particularly annoyed with those with lofty titles in companies who give the smug look, a quick nod, and fail to mutter a hello. It's as if it is beneath them to utter the simple greeting.

Does this mean that you have to have a happy face and wear a "Have a Nice Day Sticker"? No, of course not. I'm just talking about a very simple hello. Do you think it makes a difference in business? If they can't show that common courtesy and respect, how can they be fun to work with or report to? Worse still, how do to they treat clients?

SET BOUNDARIES

● ● ●

We've all heard of the statement about needing to set boundaries. To me, it very simply means establishing ground rules for what you will or won't do. Basically, it's having the confidence to stick up for what you personally believe in. Boundaries can bend occasionally or have some leeway, but they really can't be crossed without some consequences.

In business, I see it as drawing a line in the sand. This would include being confident enough to realize it is okay to say no and that you can't do everything. You can be upfront and alert people that you don't answer emails on the weekend unless it's an emergency. Colleagues need to be aware that you leave the office at a certain hour each day. This advice may seem like common sense but it's important not to let people take advantage of your good demeanor, ability to get things done, or willingness to help out colleagues. Setting boundaries may be a simple statement but it carries a lot of weight and how you handle them and says a lot about you. Take a deep breath and do it. Establish some personal guidelines, set up the boundaries, and stick to them. You'll be respected more than you might think.

SHARE KNOWLEDGE
AND INFORMATION

● ● ●

Many people have a misguided belief that, by controlling information and not sharing knowledge, they will somehow have the upper hand over others. Perhaps because of their title within an organization, they are protective of their knowledge and give out data very selectively. People like that are not leaders. They may have some fancy business card, but the reality is that they are weak leaders. Their actions inhibit collaboration, innovation, and creativity. I'd be very wary working for an extended period of time in organizations where you feel you're working in the dark or don't have all of the information you need to make the best decisions.

Early in my sales career, I kept a lot of account information on spreadsheets, in unsophisticated databases, and even on some off-the-shelf account tracking software that I had purchased at an office supply store. I guarded the intelligence as if it was top-secret information and only belonged to me. The marketing, finance, and product development teams acted this way too. We often only shared on a need-to-know basis. This was detrimental to developing new business, better products, and doing it more profitably. Many companies were like this. Now, with the advent of such user-friendly customer relationship management software—CRMs—there's no excuse for not sharing and collaborating. However, I still hear about this issue in many companies.

The companies who guard and control information from their teams will quickly find themselves falling behind the competition. They will also lose capable employees who will become frustrated, feel their careers stagnated, and vision dimmed by the lack of knowledge. The best leaders share information, are transparent with the numbers, and encourage everyone at all levels to be fully knowledgeable of the business. You want to work with those leaders and at those companies.

SHOULD YOU HAVE A
PERSONAL WEBSITE?

● ● ●

Just a few years ago, I didn't think that most people needed
a personal website. I thought it was an ego-fueled wish and
just another online venue that you had to update and monitor.
However, I've changed my view, and now think that many
people can benefit from having their own website. It's a simple
way to illustrate your skills and share experiences. It can be an
excellent supplement to your LinkedIn or Instagram efforts.

How could you feature your artistic work or your writing?
If you're a programmer, a marketer, or have other expertise,
how can you share your talents? You can get ideas by looking at
other websites for some people in your field.

SINCERITY

• • •

This is a word that describes a quality that I think carries so much weight. How would you describe it when someone says, "Sincerity"? For me, words such as honorable, truthful, reliable, and trustworthy all come to mind. A sincere person is thought of as genuine and authentic. Being known as sincere in both your personal and business life is a goal you should have.

For some people, exhibiting sincerity comes naturally; these people are caring, honest, and are thoughtful listeners. However, others find they need to work on having their quality, perhaps after they've had 360 review feedback. They may also have a good manager who helps them enhance this ability or they hire a coach who can offer techniques to improve their sincerity. Much like the skills of emotional intelligence, we all possess sincerity, but it can require a conscious effort to develop it and continually improve.

Unfortunately, we all know people whose egos and selfishness blind them to the importance of sincerity. I think the best colleagues to work with and great leaders to work for possess true sincerity. Take the time to learn from feedback you get from assessments. Listen to subtle hints from colleagues that you may not fully be authentic in your work or communication. Sincerity is not a weakness; it's a quality demonstrated by those with confidence, genuine respect for others, and a foundational building block for our character.

SOCIAL SKILLS AND SOFT SKILLS ARE SO IMPORTANT

● ● ●

Soft skills and social skills are qualities that help you work and interact with others in a positive way. Soft skills such as work ethic, showing empathy, believing in yourself and emotional intelligence are qualities often not taught in schools or colleges, but in my opinion, they should be required courses. It's assumed that people understand and learn these aptitudes on their own but that is often not the case.

Some people always exhibit these skills while others have no idea how their lack of this aptitude reflects on them in a negative way. It doesn't matter if you've got a lofty corporate title or advanced degrees, you can still be deficit in soft skills and social skills.

There is no doubt that formal training in management, gaining technical expertise, or staying current with social media marketing are critical to learn depending on your job. However, I feel that spending time to improve our social skills and soft skills can only pay us back in dividends by making us better businesspeople and individuals. I believe these skills are essential to learn and critically important if we are to be successful.

SPECIAL EVENTS—
HALF DAYS OR
GROUP FUNCTIONS

● ● ●

Through the years, I've been fortunate to have worked for managers and companies that would surprise us every so often with a message to leave a bit early. Often times, it was before a holiday weekend, but the random occasions, often in the summer, were met with an enthusiastic response. Let's face it, on the first warm spring Friday, we're distracted anyway, so letting people sneak out a few hours early isn't going to cost the business a whole lot. It's a simple gesture, but it's always appreciated by everyone and I think its impact on the corporate culture is significant. Of course, these perks need to apply to all employees, not selectively.

The other concept that I've always admired was the picnics, corporate outings, or holiday parties. Obviously, these events can be costly and, if held during working hours, there is an impact on the business. However, I think the payback in good will and positive feedback is substantial. That said, there is always a small percentage in every group who ask, "Do I have to go? Can I just take the day off instead?" I would always groan when I'd hear those people say that and shake my head in disbelief. There are always those who just can't enjoy the nice offering.

If you're managing a group of people, look for ways to offer small gestures like these. Maybe have pizza brought in for your department every so often. Order lunch from the local food truck. Schedule a happy hour with non-alcoholic drinks along with beer and wine.

These special events can make people feel good, appreciated, and become a part of the overall positive culture that you want to create.

SPEND TIME, BE SEEN, AND REACH OUT TO THE PEOPLE YOU MANAGE

● ● ●

If you're managing a staff, you will inevitably be spending some time with each person over the course of the workweek. You may have a regular department meeting, a one-on-one check-in, or maybe a session to review a specific project. These interactions are simply part of your responsibility as manager.

However, on occasion, over the course of my career I have heard about managers who rarely communicated with their direct reports outside of required meetings. People would tell me that their manager would immediately go into his or her office first thing in the morning without greeting staff or not talking to a staffer outside of a scheduled meeting time. No one wants a micro manager, but we all want someone who is accessible and visible.

On the other hand, I'm really irked by the VP, Senior VP, CEO or anyone else with a lofty title who struts around showing everyone how important he or she is. We know you've got a big job, but that doesn't mean that you have to act like you're unapproachable.

I've been pretty lucky to work in corporations where most of the senior leaders didn't act that way. There were a few who acted as if others were invading their space in elevators or they didn't have time to acknowledge employees in the hallway.

One place where you learn a lot about people is the cafeteria. Watch how people with fancy titles behave. Do they say hello to the cashier and greet people in the coffee line? Are they talking to their peers as well as the entry level staff?

The real leaders are those who reach out to everyone in an organization and makes people feel they are a part of the team and respected no matter what position they have. As you grow in your career, make sure you always treat people the right way.

SPRING CLEANING— KEEP YOUR WORK STATION ORGANIZED AND CLUTTER-FREE

● ● ●

Through the years, this became somewhat of a joke for my colleagues; I would often recommend an office cleaning, document deletion, and general purge of accumulated stuff.

I called it a business "spring cleaning." I find that deleting old files on my computer and tossing out stuff that's piled up in my office is a chance to regroup and reorganize. I've done this twice a year, usually a day around Christmas and also around July 4th, which are traditionally quieter business weeks. This "spring cleaning" may not be for everyone but I've really found it helpful as it reinforces for me the objective of focusing on key tasks and purging things that get in the way.

Some people seem to be able to manage with a desktop monitor screen cluttered with dozens of Word and Excel files, photos, Apps, and PowerPoint presentations all cluttered about. Their work station has reports and other old material piled up. I'm not one of those people. How about doing some "spring cleaning" around the next big holiday?

STAYING CURRENT
WITH SKILLS
NEEDED FOR THE
FUTURE

● ● ●

This entry is related to the other entries related to life-long learning. Think back to the skills you had after you completed high school or college and how much work has changed since then. From technology to marketing techniques to leadership styles to how much we can learn online, virtually everything we do involves new skills.

What do you need to learn to continue to be successful in your profession far into the future? The answers will determine whether you'll be successful or fall behind. How do you keep current? What are the skills that you will need to enhance to remain on top of your game? What new proficiencies do you need to master? Over the course of my career, I have always asked myself those questions and I have tried to focus on new developments along with gaining expertise with techniques, technology advancements, and new approaches to doing my work better.

LinkedIn regularly has posts and reports noting the skills needed by profession for the future. You can track them there with the hashtag #FutureSkills. The skills that people flag cover the gamut, from the ongoing need to improve social skills to using artificial intelligence. Here's a list that's from the World Economic Forum listing the top skills we'll need in 2020.

1. Complex Problem-Solving
2. Critical Thinking
3. Creativity
4. People Management
5. Coordinating with Others
6. Emotional Intelligence
7. Judgement and Decision-Making
8. Service Orientation
9. Negotiation
10. Cognitive Flexibility

The bottom line is that you need to keep your focus on the skills needed for future and not be complacent, thinking that what you've mastered today will remain relevant three years, five years, or ten years down the road. The skills will undoubtedly change and you have to keep up.

STAYING UP-TO-DATE WITH TECHNOLOGY AND SOFTWARE

● ● ●

When the Blackberry mobile device was first released in 1999–2000, my employer at the time ordered some for selected people to test. I was one of the lucky ones. I thought I was so cutting-edge as I used it for telephone calls, emails, and internet searches. It used to have an auto message added to every email saying that "This has been sent by a Blackberry" to let everyone know you had this new toy. I remember being on airplanes and other businesspeople actually marveling at it and being a bit jealous as I used it.

A few years later, everyone seemed to have one and then people moved on to iPhones, Samsung, and other Android devices. I continued to upgrade my Blackberry, but they fell behind the times, and then, instead of being on the cutting edge, I had the out-of-date, small black handheld device.

Desktops, laptops, tablets, mobile devices, and all technology tools seem to go through an evolution every three years. Anyone still buying flash drives? It can get expensive to always buy the new upgrade, the new electronic watch, or the latest gadget, so I'm not saying you need to buy them, but don't fall behind the times with new tech.

The same holds true with software and apps. They are constantly getting better and more advanced. You'll definitely fall behind other colleagues and the competition if you're not embracing a new CRM, a better account management system, or financial tracker. This is true whether you're new to the business or a more seasoned professional.

Don't say, "What I use now works just fine. Why do I need to change?" Sign up for the training classes, seek out the new tools, and you will be current, professional, and marketable.

SWOT ANALYSIS
—BUSINESS

● ● ●

A number of years ago, I attended a seminar led by a former executive at several Fortune 1000 companies. He had a very impressive track record and was discussing his views on leadership and decision-making. He spoke of some major moves his employers made and the process involved that included off-site meetings, executive team all-day sessions, and even hiring consultants at times to help formulate decisions. His main point was that leaders often complicate matters. He told us his favorite—and often most productive—tool for a quick examination of his business was the SWOT Analysis.

This key advice stood for Strengths, Weaknesses, Opportunities, and Threats. I was perplexed at the time but, as it turns out, that advice was so useful that I've used SWOT analyses many times for business decision-making. SWOT analyses are done without a lot of fanfare; it's not intimidating. It is great for working as part of a team and helpful for preparing an outline if more in-depth review is needed. Here are some example bullet points for each:

- Strengths:
  - Our company has a strong reputation in the marketplace.

- o The innovative efforts from the product development group have consistently given us a leg up on the competition.

⌂ Weaknesses:
- o We just don't have the expertise in this field.
- o Given our size, there are customers to whom we can't provide enough attention.

⌂ Opportunities:
- o The marketplace is healthy and continuing to expand.
- o Our competition is faced with some cutbacks due to issues with other markets they're in.

⌂ Threats:
- o Our competition is expanding rapidly with both an increased sales team and product offering.
- o If the stock market slumps, some of our key accounts could cut spending and investment.

There are so many advantages to doing a SWOT analysis. In a relatively painless way, you can create a document with clear messages. When you then add in the financial reports for your department, the true state of your business, pro and con, is very evident. I also like the aspect of bringing in others to be a part of the process, as it fosters a team approach. A SWOT analysis is a terrific way to develop an honest assessment of your business.

SWOT ANALYSIS—
PERSONAL

● ● ●

In one form or another, throughout the course of our careers we have all heard this question, "Do you know what your strengths and weaknesses are?" It really is the simplest of questions but, more often than not, we hem and haw, giving a few lame positives and then shuffle our feet as we rattle off some of our weak characteristics. I think the personal SWOT analysis is an excellent tool for focusing on our Strengths, Weaknesses, Opportunities, and Threats. Throughout my time in the corporate world and now as a career and executive coach, I have found that you can learn a lot about yourself and others by spending time reviewing these four qualities. We reveal a lot about our confidence level, the ability to be honest and candid, along with demonstrating how willing we are to learn new skills and how open we are to improvement.

The exercise often breaks down barriers and enables people to reveal things about themselves. It helps me learn so much more about my clients and then we can explore ways of adapting, refining, or altering their current methods, if it is appropriate, or they want to make adjustments. More often than not with my clients, I need to reinforce the need to focus more on their strengths and not let weaknesses slow them down.

You can do this yourself too. All it takes is a sheet of paper or your computer to start jotting down notes and reviewing them every so often to see what's changed, what's improved, or what remains an issue. I also believe working with a coach to review your findings is well worth the investment in time and money. If your employer has a learning and development department, that is a good place to start. The personal SWOT analysis is an inexpensive yet very effective self-improvement exercise.

TAKE A PUBLIC
SPEAKING CLASS

● ● ●

We've all heard that the number one fear that most people have is speaking in public. We're afraid of making a mistake, forgetting what we want to say, or are simply terrified that we'll make a fool of ourselves. We lose sleep over it, our stomachs churn, our mouths go dry, and our legs shake as we prepare to speak in front of people, whether we're in a conference room with ten colleagues or at a podium in front of hundreds of people. Public speaking is torture for the vast majority of employees.

I've spoken in front of small and large audiences throughout my career. No matter how many times I've done it, I can still feel my stomach tighten up before I start. I don't believe people who say they never get nervous speaking in public. It's a normal reaction that impacts everyone.

However, I think the solution to overcoming fear and nervousness is practice and forcing yourself to get in situations where you have to speak. Don't immediately volunteer to speak to two hundred people but get more experience by speaking in front of smaller groups. To be successful in business, you're going have to learn how to master this to some degree. I recommend taking a public speaking class at a local college or even short-term courses offered at a local high school or community center.

You should expect that you're always going to be a little nervous. For me, my solution is to plan, prepare, and practice my entire presentation, but I focus on my opening and the first two minutes to get me started and that gets me comfortable. I never write out an entire speech. I just speak from bullet points. Take a public speaking class and raise your hand to speak in a meeting or two. Believe me, it will help you immensely.

TAKE ACTION:
YOU CAN DO IT!

• • •

If you just sit quietly and never participate, never raise your hand, never offer to help someone else, or just never join in, you're going to miss out on so much and, consequently, you'll often feel isolated. You may even gradually lose confidence in yourself and find it even harder to participate. Instead of being part of a team or a cause, you'll be stuck in a pattern of not taking any action at all.

Now, candidly, there are times when I love just sitting back, not doing a thing, and being by myself. I think it's good for everyone to occasionally be by themselves. However, I don't think that should be the norm. We all need to step up and participate. Ask to join a group to solve a problem, volunteer to assist a colleague who needs a hand, or be the one to gather the group together to develop a new idea. It's called taking action. Take a deep breath. You know you can do it if you put your mind to it. You'll feel better about when you do and the personal rewards will inspire you to do it more often.

TAKE ADVICE
AND LISTEN TO
OPINIONS

• • •

Receiving advice from a colleague or getting someone's opinion are really two different things. Advice is a suggestion, guidance, or recommendation you may receive from a friend, manager, or coworker. An opinion is a person's view, judgement, or assessment of something.

One similarity is that sometimes we're just not in the mood to hear or read someone's thoughts about us or our work. There's that old line, "If I wanted your advice or opinion, I would have asked for it!" The word "asked" is the key one. We often don't ask, but we get it anyway.

It's human nature to get a bit thin-skinned at times or not really want to hear someone's feedback that may not be exactly to our liking. However, you should check your ego at the door, don't be stubborn, and listen to what others have to say. If the advice or opinion surprises you, then get feedback from someone else to confirm or reconfirm the information you've heard. The end result will, more often than not, make you a better employee and person in the long run.

We've all worked with people who give their opinions on everything and they believe their views are "always right." You have two options to deal with these people: You could snap back and get into an endless back and forth of arguing and end up looking just as bad as the offensive one. The other approach is to listen, say thanks for the guidance, tell the individual you'll take it under consideration, and give a subtle nod or smile. You'll look like a leader if you follow that path.

TAKE CONTROL OF YOUR OWN DESTINY

● ● ●

A t the end of the day, you have to look out for yourself and take control of your own destiny. I don't mean to sound negative, but the reality is that you are the one who can dictate what decisions you make, what direction you want to take, and what next steps make the most sense for you to be happy and fulfilled. This is true for both our personal and professional lives.

In the business world, we often get complacent or assume that someone is looking out for us. I've actually been very lucky to have reported to people through the years who have protected their teams. They ensured that when opportunities became available, they supported their staff to get those positions. However, I've heard from other colleagues about situations where their managers didn't do that. They were fair-weather friends, so to speak.

The most common example I hear in my work as a career coach are situations when people write or call former coworkers and ask for a job lead or assistance in finding a new position. People who were once connections and work friends turned out to be just no more than acquaintances. They don't respond to those reaching out and requesting assistance. It's the sad reality that I often repeat to people that our sphere of real friends or those you can count on is lot smaller that we all think.

Again, it's a bit of a downer to be so blunt with this, but it does reinforce the point that human nature is that most people just worry about their own interests. However, it's what they do next that separates the good people from those who you can't count on. Do they come to support you and provide assistance, or go on without you? This is why I believe you need to make decisions based on what makes sense for you and you have to take control of your own destiny.

That said, I would hope you always remember to help others who need it, be there to lend a hand, provide encouragement, and not be turn your back or ignore those who reach out to you.

THANK-YOU NOTES

● ● ●

This is was something I learned from my mother and it's just stuck with me through the years. She required my brother, sister, and I send thank you letters after we got Christmas gifts, birthday presents, or received something special.

I always found it such a chore to write the three-line note saying it was a great present. I'm a bit embarrassed to admit that, one Christmas, I wrote a dozen or so thank you notes in mid-December. (My focus on planning and preparation started early in my life.) At my desk in my bedroom I wrote:

"Dear _____,

Thank you so much for the great gift, I plan to _____(wear/use/play with) it every day. Hope to see you soon.

Love, Dean"

I'm not sure that's what my mom had in mind, but I think it was a hit with my relatives, who appreciated my ingenuity and, I guess to some degree, my "sincere" thank you letter.

In business, I've always sent some type of note following a business meeting with a client, customer, or a new contact. In the old days, I would send a printed letter and then went to email when that became standard practice. However, more often than not, I still print it out and snail mail it. Through the years, you would be amazed at the reactions this old-fashioned approach got from people and the number of times, years later, the recipients would show me that they had kept the note I had sent.

It takes a few minutes of time, yet it conveys such positive feedback, and has a long-term impact. We all know of one or two friends who have those special note cards or pads of paper with their names on it, yes? Give it a try.

Note: To this day, it's considered standard practice to send a written follow-up note and word of thanks after a job interview.

THINK TWICE
BEFORE SENDING
THAT EMAIL

● ● ●

Have you ever gotten an email that gets the hair up on the back of your neck? Someone has questioned your work or tossed out some unfair criticism about something you've done. It triggers a knee-jerk reaction where you want to respond immediately. You all know what I'm saying, right?

You find yourself leaning closer to the monitor, your eyes open wider, and then you mutter, "Well, how dare they? I'll show them a thing or two." You start to type at record speed, letting loose with your own brand of venom and gasoline to toss onto the fire. You barely catch your breath, and I guarantee you even find yourself hitting the keyboard a bit harder too. And then you hit "Send," with a smirk on your face saying, "Ha, that'll teach 'em!"

The next day, you've either got an email trail of back-and-forth comments that goes on for pages, or you've been called into your manager's office, or, worse yet, human resources for some conflict resolution classes. Does this sound familiar? If you've not done it personally, (Ha!) I can pretty much guarantee you've been copied on correspondences like this.

We are a society that moves at an incredibly rapid pace. In fact, we have become impatient with the speed of downloads, response times from customer service, and delivery schedules from online retailers. We want answers, or we want to give or get feedback now.

This has resulted in us responding to or sending new emails without thinking through the proper response or realizing the consequences of our quick-fingered replies. Once your words are out there, as we all know, it's pretty much impossible to reel them back in. I hope you don't think the "recall" email requests actually work!

Stepping back, evaluating the consequences, or just taking a deep breath before emailing your response is well worth doing. Next time you're furious, put your email response in the draft folder overnight, at least for an hour, or at a bare minimum, try counting to ten. Just pause and think before hitting "Enter" and sending that email.

TIME MANAGEMENT

● ● ●

There are hundreds of books on the subject of time management, along with articles online and in print. You can take seminars on the subject or watch a number of great courses on LinkedIn Learning and other video-based training sites helping you with ideas on improving your time management skills. How we manage our time is probably on the short list of issues that we all wish we could manage better.

Often, we assume that people have a firm grasp managing their time; however, through the years I've seen so many people struggle with it. The balance of handling the tasks that are a part of our job descriptions, deadlines to complete projects, emails to write or respond to, follow-up with our managers, family obligations, and just finding free time can be overwhelming.

When we first started our business careers, most of us received some type training for our job, whether we worked in sales, marketing, or finance. We probably sat in a class on using our company's technology and we had to take an orientation from human resources. However, how many of you had to take a time management training class?

This is an issue so critical to our success, happiness, and effectiveness at work that I think some time management training and coaching should be required for all employees. You need to take the initiative to find ways to improve, whether you're just beginning your career or have worked for several (or many) years. The following entries are a few tips I have used to help me manage and focus my responsibilities. You shouldn't attempt to do all of these, since that would then take up your whole day! However, I would urge you to try a few and then seek out specific training to meet your needs. They are well worth your investment.

TIME MANAGEMENT— SET TIMELINES AND FIRM DEADLINES

● ● ●

We so often hear people say, "Let's meet in a few weeks," or, "How about we follow up on that in a couple of days?" or, "I really liked your presentation, let me get back to you next month," and my favorite, "Let's take that offline." Then days and weeks go by and nothing happens. There's no follow-up, no next meeting, and whatever momentum there was has now waned.

A similar issue happens when you have a project or presentation scheduled for a date in two or three weeks and you find yourself in a mad rush completing everything two days or—heaven help me—the night before it's due.

We've all had this happen. We've all had that last-minute panic. Yes, it's even happened to me, who have preached the importance of meeting deadlines and setting timelines. Sometimes you're just procrastinating and avoiding tasks that may be too painful to complete. I always waited until the eleventh hour to complete the quarterly reports that most of my employers required. For years, I'd have to drag myself to the computer and tie myself down to get them done on time.

The solution to procrastination and last-minute rushing: set dates, timelines and deadlines for follow-up, meetings, new appointments, reports that are due or any other required work. It's really just a simple nonthreatening one-liner to add to a conversation or the notes to a meeting, "Let's get a date in the calendar," or, "How about we agree on a date for the follow -up meeting?"

I put due dates, start dates, and deadlines in my calendar for anything I feel is important. It's a strategy that has worked for me. Try it for yourself.

TIME MANAGEMENT— YOUR MOST PRODUCTIVE TIMES TO COMPLETE WORK

● ● ●

Do you know your most productive times of the day? What are the times when you're really not working at 100 percent? Aligning your productive times with your most important projects seems like an obvious move, but you would be surprised at how often that doesn't happen. You get sidetracked by an email, someone stopping by your work station, or a meeting goes past its scheduled end time. The next thing you know, that important project you really want to devote time to has been relegated to a slot on your calendar when you're not fully energized to focus on it.

You already know what those times are, but it's a good practice to track your work over a period of a few days or a week and do a quick analysis of when you did things. Then, separately, jot down your view of when you think you do your most effective work.

For me, my best times have been pretty consistent throughout my career. Here's the review of my best and weakest times of the day:

- 🗂 8:00 a.m.–10:00 a.m.
  - ○ 100 percent effectiveness
  - ○ Unlike some people, I really am a morning person and I've always tried to work on my most important projects or critical tasks in this two-hour window.

- 🗂 10:00 a.m.–12:00 p.m.
  - ○ 80 percent effectiveness
  - ○ Perfect for meetings, as I've faded a bit, but I'm still on my toes for discussions, reviews, and one-on-one sessions.

- 🗂 12:00 p.m.–2:30 p.m.
  - ○ 60 percent effectiveness (I may be too generous)
  - ○ I've always tried to use this time slot for email, administrative tasks, and anything that doesn't require me to make major decisions. Maybe it's food from lunch or the coffee that's worn off from the morning. I just don't feel as sharp.

- 🗂 2:30 p.m.–5:00 p.m.
  - ○ 75 percent effectiveness
  - ○ Good times for meetings, follow-up with colleagues, conference calls, and so forth.

- 🗂 At home after dinner:
  - ○ 85-90 percent effectiveness
  - ○ When I've had work that I had to complete from home, that hour or so without interruption has always been a very productive one for me.

Try out this exercise and then keep it mind as you plan and schedule your own work activities.

TIME MANAGEMENT— FIND THIRTY MINUTES A DAY TO REGROUP & REENERGIZE

● ● ●

You've probably heard this advice before and, unfortunately, most people just don't do it. However, I think it's so critically important to find time each day to stop, regroup, and reorganize. Simply said, it's clearing your head. We all have excuses about meetings that run back-to-back all day, or we just don't have time to break away from out desks for thirty minutes. Then find fifteen minutes or, at least, take a five-minute walk away from your desk.

Ironically, for me, this has proven to be an invaluable use of my time not just to refresh myself, but to sort out ideas or clarify what I want to do for next steps on a project. Sometimes we just can't find these breaks in our schedules to do this, and that's okay. However, if there's no time to slot this in during three out of five work days, then that's a red flag that you've got time management issues to solve.

Look at your calendar right now and plug in some times over the next week to regroup and reenergize during the course of your day. I guarantee it will make a difference.

TIME MANAGEMENT— THE FIRST THING YOU'RE GOING TO DO ON MONDAY MORNING

● ● ●

I think we all need to have a plan for the start of every day of the week, but this is especially true for Monday morning. Monday sets the tone for the entire week and, if you get things going positively at the beginning of the week, then your momentum is moving in the right direction right from the beginning.

Over the years, I've seen people lose precious time and motivation from not having a strategy for getting things underway first thing Monday morning. I see this as an easy, yet critical, step for the successful businessperson. Do it each week and see what a difference it makes.

TIME MANAGEMENT— TAKE TWENTY MINUTES ON FRIDAY TO PREPARE FOR THE UPCOMING WEEK

● ● ●

I think a great exercise to help keep tasks manageable is one where you focus specifically on the plan for the upcoming week. I recommend you take twenty to thirty minutes before your week ends on Friday to lay the framework with an action plan and scheduling session for the upcoming five days.

The first thing we need to do is ensure that we are scheduling our most important work during times when we are most productive. Do a quick review of what you did during the past week and when you did it. You'll often find that you spent too much time on email correspondence or administrative tasks and then realize that you're doing your most important work at 4:30 in the afternoon or your least productive time of the day.

Each of us will have a list that may consist of critical follow-up to be done, action items that need attention, planning and preparation for key meetings, and the essential tasks that are a part of our job descriptions.

No matter what our job is, we'll have administrative responsibilities and the emails that come in every day that can bog us down but are still important for us to handle. These can be done during times when we may not be at 100 percent efficiency. It's also important to leave free time available for opportunities that may arise to solve a problem or just catch our breath. I want to leave the office on Friday with a clear vision of what needs to be done so I can begin the new week, ready to go first thing Monday morning.

So, if I walked into your office right now and asked, "What are the first three things you're going to do Monday morning?" would you have the answer?

Organizing our tasks and responsibilities into manageable pieces is so critical; it helps eliminate the feeling of being over-whelmed and it helps keep our tasks focused. Take that time late in the day this and every Friday to map out your upcoming week with a twenty to thirty-minute scheduling and action plan session. You'll be glad you did.

TIME MANAGEMENT— PLAN FOR THIRTY DAYS, NINETY DAYS, SIX MONTHS, ONE YEAR, EIGHTEEN MONTHS

● ● ●

Early in my career, I remember that my employers would talk about three year and five-year strategic plans with details on the direction they wanted our organization headed. They were elaborate plans that needed to be updated and revised regularly. Today, since business changes far more rapidly, these multi-year strategic plans generally become obsolete and meaningless very quickly.

My personal difficulty in focusing too far in the future is probably because of my career in sales. With your sales forecasting and budgeting perspective, you often view six months into a new calendar or fiscal year, which takes you out eighteen months. Candidly, I think an eighteen-month plan is perfect for most businesspeople since it keeps you focused, organized, and realistic with expectations.

You've already read my views on making plans for the upcoming week. Now I'm starting with plans for the next month, three months, and so on. The details in the thirty-day plan are obviously more thorough so you understand the process.

The monthly plan covers all of our critical responsibilities for our job, regardless of our position. It includes time for planning and preparation, internal meeting schedules, and other preplanned events. We should have a clear vision of the month ahead, which will enable us to keep focused, have an action plan, and know well in advance if we need to call for extra support or have any timeframes adjusted.

After the thirty-day framework is mapped out, you then need to look at the quarter which will include various administrative updates for your managers, reviews with other departments or colleagues, and other regularly scheduled items.

The half year, full year, and eighteen months plan is where you can focus on the three to five key initiatives that aren't just required for management, but they will really help you grow your business. Part of your list will include budgeting, but you may also have added an objective of expanding new opportunities, cultivating projects that are showing promise, or allocating an additional 10 percent of time and energy to invest more in items that can pay increased dividends.

This prep work won't eliminate all the hassles of time management but doing so will make it far less likely that you'll be facing last-minute crunches and unfinished work.

TIME MANAGEMENT— BREAK THINGS DOWN INTO MANAGEABLE PIECES

● ● ●

Through the years, I've spent a lot of time focusing on the skills of prioritizing and scheduling key responsibilities with my teams. There are a number of important practices that you can use to help avoid time-wasting tasks and ensure that the critical items are handled first.

The feeling of being overwhelmed or not knowing where to start can be solved by breaking tasks down into smaller manageable pieces. We've all been there and often have times when balancing the needs and requests from all colleagues, managers, and clients can be more than a little overwhelming. It's so important to prioritize your tasks and focus on what's truly important for your work and your company if you are to grow the business. This applies whether you're just starting your career or are a more seasoned professional.

Prioritizing our tasks and responsibilities into manageable pieces is critical. Doing so lets you focus on the work that will have the most impact and you're less likely to be inundated. Taking the time to organize and prioritize is a vital skill set of a successful business professional. I can assure you that the time and energy you give it is an excellent investment.

TO-DO LISTS CAN BE HELPFUL

● ● ●

There has been a lot of discussion about the value or lack of "To-Do" lists. Some people end up being controlled by the lists and spend more time creating them than actually getting things done.

My view is that you need to be organized with any work that needs to be accomplished and focused on the tasks with the greatest priority. A two-page list of things to do is not the answer.

However, having your key five or six items flagged and listed so that your energy is targeting them for action is a wise strategy to follow. I think that focused approach for the list is sensible.

TRAINING TO LEARN
HOW TO DISMISS
AND LET PEOPLE GO

• • •

For any manager, letting someone go has to be one of the worst things you'll have to do. There's just nothing pleasant about it. There are a variety of reasons why you have to let someone go. Perhaps someone has been underperforming; you've given the person warnings and time to reverse his performance, which reflects poorly on you too. Perhaps you didn't hire the right candidate, or you did a weak job of training and leading. Or you may have to let someone go when the markets change and you need to downsize. That's so painful, since it really is not the impacted person's fault at all. Maybe the only time when it's easier to let someone go is when the reasons involve insubordination, ethical business standards abuse, or any form of harassment or discrimination.

As a coach, I've met a number of people who have lost their jobs. I'm amazed at some of the stories I've heard. One individual said he had recently been let go from his company after eighteen years because of "expense-saving measures." He then felt like an outcast and was even given the cold shoulder by his manager during his final few days at his office. I have heard some real horror stories of what people have been told during dismissal meetings or how they were treated when their job was eliminated. Frankly, it can really make your head shake at the poor leadership skills.

I have seen how some human resources professionals have handled very difficult downsizing circumstances. They have taught me a lot and modeled the way to enable me to improve at the communication process and show real compassion when I have had to let people go. I believe that the vast majority of HR professionals know how to handle this critical skill, although I know some of you may disagree.

Letting someone go takes training that may not be offered at all companies. I am not talking about four weeks or a semester of intensive classes; I am thinking about a half-day program or workshops over a few evenings. However, I also think the training needs to be retaken and reviewed every few years so that we are always improving. I think every manager should be required to receive this training and you should seek it out if you manage people.

TRANSPARENCY

● ● ●

What does it mean for a person or a company to be transparent? To me, I think it is an important quality that separates people and companies with whom I want to work from the rest of the pack. Transparency links closely to authenticity—being genuine, honest, and open. You're letting people see you for what you are, what you believe in, and not masking anything with phoniness or ego.

Transparent companies create a culture where everyone feels involved and part of the overall mission. Transparency not only means sharing information but explaining what it all means too. Executives must let down their guard and share their plans and thinking with employees. You must help educate everyone at a company to help create a winning environment.

Situations like this foster more open dialogues, offices with more communication, and the sharing of ideas. If you've ever worked in a department or a company where you had no idea what the mission was, where the new opportunities would develop, or if business was good or bad, you know how frustrating and distressing that can be for employees. The same applies if you report to people who aren't transparent. Work can be tortuous if you are always trying to figure out what your manager means or what he's thinking. You'll always be on edge and not focused on the objectives. This type of situation fosters an environment of "us vs. them," rather than teamwork. Work on being transparent, genuine, and authentic. Being open and real actually makes life easier since you're not trying to be someone you're not.

TREATING
EVERYONE WITH
RESPECT

● ● ●

You can learn so much about a person by watching how he or she interacts with people who have different job titles. Does he show the same respect to the office assistant as he does do to the senior executive? Does he smile and greet the receptionist or treat them as a support person? Treating people equally would seem to be so easy to do, yet some people just can't grasp this concept.

I take pride that I knew the parking garage guys in my building by name, the nice ladies who were the cashiers in the cafeteria, and that I could always count on a warm smile and a hug from the receptionist on the executive floor. It was a mutual respect that made all of us feel good.

Treating people with respect is equally important in the office as well as in our day-to-day lives. Do you greet the waiter, thank the doorman, and show appreciation to those in any service position? Again, you can learn a lot by just observing others in similar situations. Several years ago, I was on a business trip and would be joining a number of other colleagues for a meeting at a hotel. I arrived late in the evening and someone I knew was checking in at the front desk, but he didn't see me. This person was complaining about the room he got and was treating the front desk clerk so poorly. I cringed when he said,

"Well, my name is Mr. X and I'm a senior vice president." To this day, I wish I had yelled out, "Who cares?" When he left, and I approached the clerk, I apologized profusely on behalf of our company. The clerk smiled and said that "Mr. X" was clearly the exception out of everyone she had met from our organization. My view of that SVP was never the same after that day.

Treating people with respect regardless of their position or job title should be second-nature for all of us. It's comes down to basic decency and being a good person. More than likely, you don't need to be reminded of these traits, but I thought it was worth including here.

TRUST

• • •

This is such a powerful word and I could find a million quotes to explain why. One of my favorites, and one that I think nails it perfectly, is this one: "Trust takes years to build, seconds to break, and forever to repair."

Think about that in a business setting. Are there colleagues or connections in whom you have lost your trust? Are there those with whom who you have let it slip away? Trustworthiness is another one of those qualities that goes to the core of who we are as individuals. You can have a lofty title, an advanced degree, or be in a position of authority, but if you're not trusted, then you are really at the bottom of the credibility ladder. Be honest, credible, authentic, maintain your character at the highest level, and be a person whom people always trust. That is worth its weight in gold.

VACIONS

● ● ●

Depending on how long you've been with a company, the job title, or the industry you're in, vacation time can vary from ten days to twenty days to a year or more. Some people are really good at making sure they use up all of their days. However, the majority of workers don't use their full allocation of vacation time. According to a recent Glassdoor survey, only 23 percent of employees are taking all of their eligible time off. The average employee takes about half (54 percent) of his or her vacation time.

We've all read about the importance of getting away from our jobs and the value of refreshing and reenergizing so that we're better workers when we come back, yet the majority of people still leave a lot of vacation time unused. I can talk all I want about the physical and mental benefits of time off and I'm sure you'll nod your head and agree with me. But if you're one of the people who never uses all your vacation days, you probably aren't listening. If you rarely take vacations, try to shift your approach slowly. Try to increase your time off by four or five days, though. Maybe take a few extra Fridays off in the summer or add a day or two near the holidays. Our companies and our work will survive without us and, if there's an emergency, you already know that we're all connected electronically. So, make the concerted effort that, this year, you'll increase the amount of vacation you've earned and actually use it.

VALUE OF A MENTOR

● ● ●

It's probably good to explain the difference between a coach and a mentor. You hire a coach for a short period of time to help you improve some skills. You may work with a coach for one, three, five, or more sessions, but there's an end date to the relationship. On the other hand, if you're lucky enough to connect with a mentor, it is someone you can learn from and work with to enhance your development for hopefully many years.

Being a mentor or being the mentee takes work and a lot of commitment. You just don't walk up and ask him to be your mentor. It requires some time to cultivate and ensure that it will be fruitful for both individuals.

I've learned from informal mentorships by tracking someone I admire by looking at how they lead people, run meetings, make decisions, or motivate their teams. They have a special quality to be able to "Model the Way." Just by observing how they've handled certain situations, I have gained so much.

However, if you want to take it to the next level and establish a more formal mentor relationship, you need to have a conversation with the other person. He or she needs to be willing to take on responsibility, since this is not just a casual relationship. A good mentor is honest, takes interest in your development, challenges you, and, although supportive, is not always patting you on the back. As a mentee, you also need to accept constructive criticism, be receptive to the tasks assigned, and be a good listener.

It's easier said than done to find a mentor, but start by tracking people you really respect in leadership roles or other positions. There's such real value in having a mentor if you're fortunate enough to make the right connection.

WHAT DOES
CHARACTER MEAN?

• • •

This is a short entry but one that carries a lot of weight. I want you to digest it and think about it again after you read this.

Dictionary.com defines character as: "The aggregate of features and traits that form the individual nature of a person." I also have used this quote from John Wooden to define it: "The true test of a person's character is what they do when no one is watching."

In my view, your character is who you really are as a person. Are you good to others? Can you be trusted? Do you care for people or just look out for yourself?

I think your character is on the short list of things that you need to protect and value at the highest level. Your peers and colleagues along with your friends and family will always respect you if your character is genuine. You also want to align yourself with others whose character is real, and they understand how important it is.

WHAT HAVE YOU DONE TO IMPROVE YOURSELF THIS WEEK?

● ● ●

Every so often, I see this question and it actually makes me feel a bit guilty that I haven't set some lofty goal of improving myself. You see it in advertisements or hear motivational speakers using it in their presentations.

I think it's a great idea to have some goal for the week ahead. However, my recommendation is that you set realistic goals. You want to make it something that you can achieve so that you have a sense of accomplishment when you complete it. Rather than saying you plan to lose weight, how about committing to go to the gym for three days? Do you want to read a book? Start with buying a book. Sign up for a class. I've always liked the objective of reorganizing or taking a step back and regrouping. For me, that's something I've done to improve myself.

We would all like to have some firm goal of enriching ourselves every week. However, I don't want that guilty feeling if I haven't accomplished something that I said I would. Give yourself something to check off the list that will make you feel good. To me, that's what the phrase means. If I improve myself, I will feel happier and more positive.

WHAT YOU SAY MATTERS (ESPECIALLY AS A LEADER)

• • •

This is such a simple statement, but you need to think about it for a minute to realize the weight that it carries. As a leader, your entire team and other colleagues listen to everything you say, watch for signs from you, and remember what you say.

I'm no longer surprised when people remind me of what I said in meetings or individually years ago. Sometimes my message was encouraging and motivating but there have also been occasions when my remarks were way off point and even misguided. I had to learn the hard way that people don't forget when, as a leader, you've made an ignorant or really dumb remark. Obviously, you want them to instead remember the positive feedback or conversations you've had.

Also, what you say matters because it often connects to a commitment or a promise you've made to a coworker, a direct report, or other colleagues. If you tell someone, "Yes, we'll review your compensation again in a few months," you can be sure that, in a few months, the person will be expecting another discussion. The same holds true if you commit to supporting someone's idea, attend a meeting, or say you'll decide by Friday. Your words matter.

In our personal lives, how many times have you said things that you wish you could have taken back? We may have let our frustration or anger get the better of us and we let out a few choice words that really hurt someone. We immediately feel ashamed or worse, knowing that our words can cut someone as bad as a knife can.

In just a few short moments, what you say and how you say it, in both positive and negative ways, can last a lifetime. So always remember to think before you speak because people are listening.

WHEN THE TEAM WINS, EVERYONE WINS

● ● ●

This entry sounds obvious, but this philosophy can make a big difference in a work setting. In my mind, there's more fun when the team wins. The culture is positive, there's collaboration, and there's a genuine feeling of comradery.

We still need to have personal goals, targets, and objectives to achieve. These are important and some individuals will perform better than others and be recognized for that.

However, when you have high performers in your organization or leaders who have that ability to take everyone under their wings, then the overall business improves. It's like a lead car drafting the cars behind it and then everyone benefits. In sports, it's the superstar who carries the heavy load, but everyone seems to do better because of them.

The culture of being part of a winning team can be powerful. I've experienced it a number of times in my career. You're working for leaders who have a vision, the marketplace is healthy, your colleagues are in sync with the mission, and there's a confidence and swagger in the hallways because people realize they're part of something that's successful.

Yes, it's great when you as an individual can stand on top of the podium or be in the winner's circle alone. However, it's even better when everyone can high five, smile, and be in a group photo marking their shared success. It's special when everyone wins, so you should strive for that.

WHEN YOU GO FOR AN INTERVIEW, YOU ARE INTERVIEWING THE COMPANY TOO

● ● ●

If you've been out of a job for a while or are anxious to leave your current employer, it is understandable that you might overlook some factors that would discourage you from pursuing a new opportunity. You want focus on the potential for new employment, an increased salary, good title, and possibly working for well-known brand/company.

However, observing the style of the interviewer, the others you will see or meet in the hallways, and just the overall "feel" of the company should be a critical part of the interview process. Are people smiling in hallways? Are people talking to one another in the elevator? How do the offices look? Is the environment clean and fresh or worn out and dreary? Are people using old or new technology?

All companies have distinct styles and cultures. Many companies even give tests to see if you will be a good fit for them. However, it should be a two-way interaction. You should also be examining a prospective employer to see whether it's the right fit for you. Sometimes you can tell from the job descriptions. You can get the feel of the personality of the company or the person who wrote the description. If you see words and phrases such as "pull no punches," "hard-hitting 24/7 style," and "aggressive, self-starter," take a moment. There's nothing wrong with these phrases, but if they don't reflect your attitude toward work, then the job may not be right for you. I've also seen job descriptions with so many responsibilities and details that my gut feeling was that the hiring manager could be a real micromanager.

Doing research about the companies where you're interviewing is also important for many reasons. You should look at the mission statement, financial results, management, but also company reviews on websites such as Glassdoor. You can also read descriptions and find out more about corporations by following them on LinkedIn.es.

The most direct examination happens during the interview itself. Whether it's with the first interviewer in human resources or with the actual hiring manager, you will learn if these are the type of people with whom you want to work. How's their personality? Do they let you speak or do they do all of the talking? Are they clear about the follow-up process?

I think you should also be wary of the types of questions they ask you. Obviously, questions about your age or sexual preference are illegal. But other, more mysterious questions can be a red flag. This peculiar question seems to be a popular one: "If you were a tree, what type of tree would you be?" I assume the point of this question is to see how you would handle a situation when you're thrown a curve ball, but this type of question seems to be too much of a game.

When you're looking for that great new job, it is human nature to overlook flaws in the companies and potential managers. However, taking a step back to ensure you are interviewing them could spare you from some disappointment down the road.

WHY DATA IS SO IMPORTANT AND VALUABLE

● ● ●

Every business professional collects an enormous amount of data. It could be costumer information, feedback about products or services, or market research gathered from a variety of sources. All of it is valuable and can be so important to running our business. However, there are three critical questions about this data:

1. What are you doing with all of this rich data and account information?
2. Where are you storing it?
3. Who has access to it?

For many years, these questions plagued organizations because there was no efficient way for sharing information and, quite candidly, many departments, were reluctant to do it. We guarded information like we owned it and only shared on a need-to-know basis. This was detrimental to developing new business opportunities, better-selling products, or innovative new services. The silos developed between departments prevented opportunities to cultivate all of this data and put it to good use to grow the business.

Data and business information needs to be shared with everyone in an organization who can put it to good use. Obviously, treating this data judiciously is essential and that needs to be reinforced regularly. However, giving access to colleagues creates an open environment which then enables everyone to feel involved and creates a sense of ownership.

Data and information are valuable on their own, but they should be used as an even more important aspect of enhancing collaboration, creative thinking, and a culture of innovation. Don't hold back data; share it wisely, but freely.

WORK AND
PERSONAL VISITS,
EMAILS, AND
TELEPHONE CALLS

● ● ●

Some companies are strict about having employee friends or relatives visit the office. Employers are also concerned with personal emails going through the corporate server and the amount of time employees spend on personal phone calls.

These matters should be handled with people using common sense and not abusing the workplace. I would hope that most managers would understand that employees will inevitably send emails to friends, take personal calls, and occasionally have friends or family visit the office. I must confess I actually loved when a colleague's parents would visit or a new mom or dad would bring in the newborn. Was is it disruptive for a little while? Yes, it was, but who cares? And the brief visit brightened everyone's day.

The problem is the habitual situation from co-workers who frequently talk loudly on a cell-phone so the entire department knows about their dating life and their health issues. There's also the person ordering items online, so the monitor is flashing the latest sale and the person's email inbox has more confirmations of personal items than business topics. You don't want to be that person in your office setting. Be smart and use common sense in your office.

WORK PERFORMANCE —360 REVIEWS

● ● ●

If you ever have the opportunity to have a 360 review, always say yes. A 360 review is an examination of your work skills and abilities compiled from feedback given by peers, direct reports, colleagues in other departments, and your manager. The 360 means there is a complete circle across the organization of people answering questions about you along with providing opinions about whether you're doing well and areas where you still need development.

The hope is that you'll have ten or more people supplying information. The more people, the better, so you won't be able to determine who said what. You will probably be able to figure out what your manager has said but the aim is for everyone to be open with feedback and the data is assembled so you get a full analysis of your work performance. Inevitably, you will focus on the skill sets that are flagged about areas in which you need improvement. It's human nature to want to figure out who passed along the real tough feedback. However, once you take the emotion out of it, you'll learn much more about yourself so you can take steps to improve.

It's nice to read positive feedback and you should accept it, and feel good about it. However, the objective is to work on those items flagged by a number of people of the areas in which you're performing below an acceptable level. In some cases, you may be surprised at the comments. I have had 360s throughout my career and have found they have helped me immensely. Even after so many years, there are areas in which I have to improve. And I continue to. As I have done 360s through the years, it's helped me immensely. I'm still a work-in-progress.

A manager or HR trainer can work with employees to review the 360s and help develop an action plan to address any bad habits or skills that need improvement.

WORK
PERFORMANCE—
APPRAISALS

● ● ●

There's no getting around it. No one likes annual performance appraisals. In fact, when handled properly, they can be an invaluable tool for both you and your manager.

The pros and cons of the appraisal process have been discussed frequently over the past few years. Many companies haven't changed this process in decades while some employers have eliminated annual appraisals. Regardless of how they're handled, most employees view them as a dreaded chore instead of opportunity to learn how they can improve or receive positive feedback about progress they've made enhancing their skills.

My theory is that the appraisal is necessary for those managers who are poor communicators because it forces them to meet with their direct reports and provide feedback. That's a pretty sad commentary but, unfortunately, in many cases, it's true.

If you're managing people now or hope to do so in the future, ongoing communication about someone's performance should be a part of the regularly scheduled check-in process with your team. Coaching and mentoring are continuous so you can easily monitor the skills, evaluate improvement, and see positive results. Personal objectives should not be forced but discussed mutually, agreed on, and regularly reviewed. Objectives need to be focused to make your direct reports more efficient, which, in turn, benefits the entire company. If these items are a part of your regular communication then the formal appraisal at the end of the year becomes a formality, not a chore.

Establish a regular timetable to discuss your performance with your manager so it doesn't become a dreaded event.

WORKING FOR A
LOUSY MANAGER

● ● ●

Lousy is a substitute for a variety of words, such as incompetent, bad, awful, or something else you might prefer. Through the years, I have become more skeptical about the quality of managers in the workplace, at large established corporations as well as small entrepreneurial businesses. Too many people have been put in management positions without having any formal training on how to actually manage people. And the concept of leading people is even farther off the radar.

Companies promote people or create positions with management titles; the person who has been promoted then assumes he has to tell staff what to do, offer criticism, and act like a boss, whatever that means.

There are many excellent managers who've learned how to motivate, provide guidance, and create a work process that enables everyone to do their jobs well. They manage and get out of people's way. However, there are so many "lousy" managers out there too. They hinder work flows, maybe intimidate, or just make their direct reports feel miserable. I've come to believe that the percentage is a lot higher than we would suspect.

What should you do if you report to one of these lousy managers? Well, every situation is different and I can only offer some general advice. You should seek guidance from your human resources contact, a coach, or a mentor who understands your specific situation. Hopefully, this person will offer some ideas on how to remedy the situation. In some cases, you can approach your manager directly and gently express the hope you can improve the current situation. Again, get guidance from someone you trust before taking any action.

However, if things do persist and you're miserable reporting to a lousy manager, then you must develop a strategy for finding a better opportunity. The line, "life is too short," definitely applies in cases like this.

WORKING FOR A
MICROMANAGER

● ● ●

No one appreciates a manager who is constantly asking about their work or looking over their shoulders.

Throughout my career, and now in my work as an executive coach, I've regularly heard about many issues that people face daily with their managers. That said, I've always tried to be very clear in saying that we need to be cognizant of the fact that the manager and employee relationship is a two-way street. We should make an honest commitment to learn to adapt to our manager's style and habits while at the same time the manager needs to understand what leadership means. However, it is alarming how people feel that they report to someone who micromanages everything they do.

It is my belief that these issues need to be addressed sooner rather than later. We need to communicate better and more directly with our managers to express our concerns diplomatically. However, we may need to accept that sometimes the answer is that we need to find a new and better opportunity with a manager at a different company. Our career, happiness, and work fulfillment are too important to let languish reporting to a micromanaging boss.

Managers need to continually improve and enhance their skills. The best managers and respected leaders have learned how to empower their teams and realize that micromanaging is a track to failure. The successful managers don't put obstacles in front of their teams; they clear a path.

Management guru Tom Peters once said, "I see the manager's principle role as identifying things that get in people's way by asking them and meticulously getting those things out of their way." If you're in a situation where your manager rarely follows that approach and you're unhappy, then it's probably time to move on.

YOU HAVE TO LEARN THE BASICS OF FINANCE

• • •

Every job has a financial aspect and, if you don't know the foundational pieces, then not only are you at a disadvantage, in my view, you're hurting your company.

Can you work your way through a P&L? Do you know what to look for on a balance sheet? Your company's income statement is a wealth of information. When was the last time you looked at it? Do you understand the terms net, gross, margin, EBITA, and what brackets around a number mean? If you are a manager, do you feel comfortable in handling the expense and departmental budgets for your department?

If you hesitate answering any of these questions, then you need to remedy the situation sooner rather than later. This is actually an easy fix. There are courses called, "Finance for Non-Financial Managers" offered at community colleges, high schools, and business organizations. There are also books and online training programs on financial basics.

Understanding finance is essential to being successful in business. It is a requirement, not an elective objective.

YOU NEED A GOOD ACCOUNTANT AND A GOOD LAWYER

• • •

We all aim to hire the best people to help us do our jobs well. However, there are two functions that are so critical to have in both your personal and business life. You need an accountant and an attorney who you can really trust. Even if you happen to be in one of those professions, having a second opinion is valuable.

It's important to have a solid understanding of finance and accounting, no matter what job you have. You should know some of the terminology, be able to read a profit and loss statement, and understand the key elements of an income statement. However, there are so many nuances to these documents, which is why people have advanced degrees in taxation or finance. The accounting professionals also keep track of the latest regulatory changes.

On the legal side, the risks are too great to attempt legal maneuvering without have the proper advice. Whether you are negotiating a settlement or preparing a business contract, you should be consulting an attorney experienced in the particular matter. The word "trust" is important, which is why I'm stressing that everyone needs an accountant and attorney whom you feel confident will help you avoid any serious harm or problems.

YOU WON'T BE
LIKED BY EVERYONE

● ● ●

It's inevitable that not everyone will like you and that can be hard for you to accept. Everyone wants to be liked, accepted, and thought of as a friend. However, life doesn't work that way. We're all different, we come from diverse backgrounds, have our own beliefs, and opinions that cover all bases. That means that there will be more than a few times you and your colleagues will be at odds. Wanting to be liked by everyone when you're in a management position can be especially frustrating. You need to understand that your job is not to be liked by everyone but help get everyone's job done successfully. If you're "liked" by some because of that, well then that's a nice plus, but that shouldn't be your objective.

You may have had a successful year in business, your efforts spilled over to help others, and you've been the life of party at a group function. There will always be someone who thinks he could have done your job better, is jealous of your results, or think your party personality is annoying.

Some people don't understand this situation at all. They completely understand that they will never be liked by everyone. They may even chuckle and say they don't want that either. However, through the years, I've worked with more than a few people who couldn't understand why everyone wasn't on their side. This entry is a reminder for those people. There will always be someone who doesn't like you. Don't worry about it.

YOUR DOCUMENTS FOLDER AND DESKTOP ON YOUR COMPUTER

● ● ●

This is another one of my entries about being organized. I know this all comes down to personal preferences about handling emails, documents, photos, and other messages that land on our computers and mobile devices. However, if you can't find something you wrote or you're searching for a document for fifteen minutes, then it's my feeling that your current organizational method isn't working.

Look at your desktop. If you can't see the screensaver because you've saved documents, programs, and photos there, that would drive me crazy. Now, review everything in your documents folder on your hard drive, network, or the Cloud. Is there any order to it? This is a perfect rainy day or late Friday spring-cleaning project. Okay, you won't hear from me again about this topic. Promise.

YOUR LANGUAGE
SAYS A LOT
ABOUT YOU

• • •

This topic may fall into my "old-school" approach, but I think it warrants some discussion. Now, I've certainly uttered a foul word every so often and there have been times when I wish I could have reeled back in an inappropriate comment or two. However, if you're known to be someone who has a salty vocabulary, that's not a badge of honor in my view.

When I was in high school and college, I worked in a restaurant. There were words and comments uttered that certainly expanded the horizon of my vocabulary. It seems restaurant kitchens have a unique language that you wouldn't tell your mother about. One of the guys I worked with went on to become a trader on Wall Street. Years later, he told me that there were days on the trading floor that reminded him of the kitchen of where we used to work. Some work environments are just that way. I'm not saying it is right; I'm just saying that it's more common and I guess people get used to it and aren't offended.

However, we all know that some words should just never be said at an office. Whether it's an F-bomb or other words that are cruel, offensive, and ugly, they are simply unacceptable at work. You know what they are and know what I mean. If you hear a colleague use one, call the person out and say that is wrong. Hear it twice, report the person without hesitation.

I've been in meetings when someone would say that a campaign was a piece of s***, or some manager was an a**hole, or at a company party, someone got really f***ed up. We've all heard the words, we're all not prudes, but know your audience, your setting, and remember that the language you use is a reflection on you as a person.

YOUR NEW JOB—
IT TAKES SIX
MONTHS TO FEEL
COMFORTABLE

● ● ●

A bit of advice I've given to people for years has been that it normally takes six months to get fully settled into a new job. I don't care if you're brand new to the business world or if you're the new CEO for a big global company. The learning curve takes time and, although it may be a bit shorter in some cases, you really should anticipate the full 180 days.

You're learning new processes, procedures, and responsibilities. With that comes the pressure of having responsibilities that you didn't have in your previous positions. You're also meeting new people, understanding which colleagues are top performers, and who are the ones who may not be thrilled you're there. Remember, other people applied for that job you're in and it may take time, if ever, for them to accept you. The manager in your old job had his own set of idiosyncrasies. Some were good and some were bad, but you knew what to expect. In your new position, while you've met your new manager during multiple interviews, you haven't seen them in stressful settings or on a grumpy Monday. You learn all this in the first week or month.

Also, it's inevitable you're going to have a bad day during the first month and a few more during the first 180 days. It may be a meltdown, some regret that you never should have left your old job, or a feeling of despair wondering if you'll ever figure it all out. Don't worry. Relax. You will. I can guarantee that everyone has those feelings at some point when they starting a new job. If people say that it's never happened to them, I'm guessing that they may be too stubborn or insecure to admit it.

If you plan on this six-month schedule, you'll be much better prepared to handle the ups and downs and manage the complete onboarding to your new position and employer.

YOUR PERSONAL BRAND

• • •

It seems like we always hear about ways to improve our "Brand." What exactly is a personal brand and why should I care?

The concept of personal branding goes back more than twenty years to an August 1997 *Fast Company* article written by Tom Peters titled, "The Brand Called You." A simple definition came from another article, "The Basics of Personal Branding" by Nick Nanton in the same publication. He wrote, "Personal branding seeks to shape the way an individual is perceived by his or her audience, whoever that audience may be."

When I work with my clients and ask what their personal brand is, I often get a blank stare in response. Then, I break it down a bit more by asking this very direct question: What do you think your peers and friends say about you when you are not around?

I know it can make you feel uncomfortable, but I think it is a great question because it forces us to think about our personal brand and goes to the core of who we are as individuals. We all have good qualities, ones that need enhancing, and others that may need some major improvement. Our brand is what people see in us and believe about us.

We are able to build and develop our personal brand by adding new skills or increasing our knowledge in certain areas. If you're a teacher, you could study advanced coding so you can be a better instructor of that subject. You could be a marketing manager and gain project management skills to help in your job. Perhaps you're an executive who needs to brush up on the basics of social media skills.

I think our personal brand starts early in our lives with what we learn from our parents or guardians, then our teachers and mentors. I'm referring to qualities and skills such as work ethic, being good to people, belief in family, authenticity, and having confidence in yourself. These traits are the foundation of our personal brand. It's our job to continue to cultivate and improve our brand throughout our lives.

YOUR PERSONAL
DESCRIPTION

● ● ●

When you meet someone for the first time and he or she asks what you do, can you respond with a clear one- or two-sentence description or do you hesitate in giving an answer? Try it for yourself right now. Imagine me standing there and asking, "So, what do for a living and what you do enjoy?" How would you respond?

You need two versions and it often comes down to common sense. The first one is what I call your description for relatives at family gatherings. You know, when everyone all gets together for a holiday. There are your family members, cousins you maybe haven't seen in ages, and some older aunt and uncles. Everyone's nice but they don't want to hear the long story about the analytical methods of digital advertising tracking. Aunt Louise wants to hear that you're in marketing in the advertising business. "Oh, that's great. Let's eat."

For business connections, you need no more than a two-sentence statement of who you are and what you do. You have to make sure it's clear and doesn't include buzzwords or jargon tied specifically to your company. You need to practice it, say it regularly, so it flows out of your mouth easily and you say it confidently. Think of yourself at a business conference and a stranger greets and introduces himself to you. Then you reply, "It is a pleasure to meet you too. I'm Jane/John Smith and, for the past two years, I've been one of the marketing directors at the XYZ Corporation here in Chicago. We're a company focused on providing the best online learning for teachers and educators."

It's short, to the point, and states who you are but leaves room for a follow-up query from the other person. "Interesting. What categories do you focus on?" "Who is your competition?" The response I really like is "How's business?" because it allows you start a conversation.

Developing a clear personal description is such simple thing to do, yet I'm always surprised how few people have one. Spend time to develop one. It's quick and easy, yet so smart to do.

YOUR PERSONAL VALUES

● ● ●

We each have unique values that we try to follow or that really matter to us. What is important to me may not even be on your list. However, values are key indicators of who we are as individuals. They also are critical ingredients of who we want to be. Values help guide you in making decisions in both your personal and business life. For me, focusing on my core values has been very helpful.

You should devote some time to isolate four or five values that drive your beliefs. You know them already, but I think it's important to write them down and focus on achieving them.

You can consult lists from online resources. Here's a group of fifty or so that I pulled from a list created by James Clear, found on jamesclear.com. Many of them are topics, in one form or another, in this book. You can add others such as family or whatever words resonate for you.

Authenticity	Achievement	Adventure
Authority	Autonomy	Balance
Beauty	Boldness	Compassion
Challenge	Citizenship	Community
Competency	Contribution	Creativity
Curiosity	Determination	Fairness

Faith	Fame	Friendships
Fun	Growth	Happiness
Honesty	Humor	Influence
Inner Harmony	Justice	Kindness
Knowledge	Leadership	Learning
Love	Loyalty	Meaningful Work
Openness	Optimism	Peace
Pleasure	Poise	Popularity
Recognition	Religion	Reputation
Respect	Responsibility	Security
Self-Respect	Service	Spirituality
Stability	Success	Status
Trustworthiness	Wealth	Wisdom

YOUR REPUTATION

• • •

What do others think about you? What do they say when you're not in the room? Do you wonder if people have certain thoughts when you're there, but when you leave, their true feelings are expressed?

Your reputation and image are developed throughout the course of your career. If your behavior or conduct ever strays, then your reputation could be tarnished and it can take years to improve it and recover it to where it once was. This quality falls in with other traits such as trust, credibility, and character. You must value and protect your reputation and ensure that you maintain it at the highest level. Never take it for granted.

YOUR VISION— DREAM BIG IDEAS

● ● ●

The ability to have vision, develop new ideas, and take them to the next stage and see them implemented is an ability that most of us don't have. Or most of us don't cultivate our vision in ways that we should.

We all have thoughts about where our business may be headed or what potential new innovations could take place, but I believe it takes a special mind and also some courage to actually try and pursue the plans for the future. We can get comfortable in the status quo; maybe we feel a bit risk averse, or just think that the concept is just too many years away.

I think a great way to think about vision is to look at people like Steve Jobs, Sheryl Sandberg, Marc Benioff, Mary Barra, and Jeff Weiner. Each of them works in different industries and, most definitely, each has unique leadership styles, but they all have an ability to set courses for their companies in innovative ways. It's worth your time to read their stories.

I have worked with people who've recently completed 360 reviews and vision is often flagged for needing development. "Does he/she project a vision for the future?" "Does he/she communicate well their vision for the company/department?" Motivating, directing the business, and other characteristics all seem to rise and fall, depending on the person, but in my unscientific study, having "vision" always seems to be lagging. (Consistently lagged on 360s for me too.)

Some people just "have it," and they are the entrepreneurs, the true visionaries. However, the rest of us need to find more time to understand it and try to let our guards down to envision where our businesses are headed. I think vision has to be cultivated. Can you give that a try and not just dream big ideas, but bring them to fruition?

YOU'VE STARTED A
NEW JOB—DAY ONE

● ● ●

This is the great equalizer. Whether you're the new SVP of Marketing, new supervisor for the Creative Team, or whatever job to fill an open position, the first day for a new hire is met with a lot of excitement and, more than likely, a few extra beats of the heart. Some nervous anticipation is natural, and it doesn't matter if you've changed jobs a lot or have been more long term in prior roles. The first day at a new job elevates your energy but may also give you a stomach full of butterflies.

Some companies handle the onboarding of new colleagues with special care and understand how important it is to have a smooth first day complete with a warm welcome. However, the majority of companies handle it poorly and, from the horror stories I've read, I don't think I'm wrong in having that opinion. It's tough to comprehend that after spending weeks or maybe even a month or more recruiting and interviewing new candidates, that the first day for a new employee is often handled poorly.

Your first day usually consists of a morning at the HR department filling out forms, getting a briefing about the company, and handling general administrative tasks. Around lunchtime, your new boss will hopefully be introducing you to colleagues in your department and then getting you settled in your work station. Don't be surprised if your computer isn't ready, your new email address isn't working yet, and more than a few people ask who you are.

Things always seem to be a bit choppy on that Monday morning of your first day. I wish it was handled better, but more often than not, there are a lot of hiccups along the way. So, take a deep a breath, smile, meet new colleagues, and begin a learning curve knowing that it will take some time to fully get a grasp on things. It can only get better after day one. I promise you.

CONCLUSION

There are about two hundred entries in this book that you just completed reading; I hope you found the guidance to be helpful. There were probably a few recommendations that you may not fully agree with, but my objective was to motivate you to think about ways of doing things better or more efficiently.

Many of the topics probably won't be in the curriculum of an MBA program or even an undergrad course in business. However, I wish more time was spent on learning and mastering these basics since I truly believe they play a critical role in achieving a successful and fulfilling career.

Looking back at my years in business I sometimes cringe, recalling how I used to do things. However, I did have a number of breakthrough moments when I learned to believe in myself, trust my instincts, and focus on improving skills that I may have taken for granted. I also know that I will always be enhancing my skills through lifelong learning so that I don't fall behind in today's fast-paced business world.

I hope you take to heart the principles and values of my philosophy. Edit my list as you feel appropriate and develop your own. It can be a great way to keep you focused with goals that enable you to be better. Write down two of your own right now.

1. Be Good to People
2. Smile and Say Hello
3. Have a Good Work Ethic
4. Send Thank You Notes
5. Always Be a Lifelong Learner
6. Confidence-Believe in Yourself
7. Integrity and Character
8. Be Authentic, Be Genuine
9. Planning and Preparation
10. Know Your Priorities, Family Comes First, and Focus on What Really Matters

You can achieve business success by learning the essential skills from this book. I hope I have provided you with the strategies for mastering the basics. I wish you happiness, good health, prosperity, and the ability to maximize your potential and opportunities.

ACKNOWLEDGMENTS

O ver the course of my career, I have been fortunate to have worked for many outstanding individuals at some terrific companies. I have learned so much not just from following their guidance, but by watching how they've managed their businesses and their interaction with others. My first manager was Gary Gutchell and those who have worked with me through the years have heard me say his name many times. The lessons he taught me both for business and my personal life guided me so well. He is the true definition of a mentor, coach, and a friend.

Many others took chances in hiring me or were instrumental recommending me for jobs. Others were at the executive levels of companies I have respected and admired. Thank you to Mike Hunter, Joe Esposito, Jack Romanos, Lee Thompson, Bill Arlington, Stephen Kippur, Steve Smith, Mark Allin, Matt Kissner, and Will Pesce.

For most of my publishing career, I worked for and with George Stanley. There aren't many better individuals than this man. He enabled me to do my job better while he handled everything else, with his non-existent ego. He has a great sense of humor, leadership style, love for his family, and his friendship extends to everyone. I've been so very fortunate to have worked with George.

My colleagues from the Professional & Trade leadership team at Wiley were very special and even with different styles we blended so well together to create a winning organization reporting to Stephen Kippur. Many thanks to Katherine Schowalter, Jeff Brown, Joe Marchetti, Larry Olson, Margie Schustack, Joan O'Neil, Elizabeth Doble, Gwen Jones, George Stanley, Debra Hunter, Kathy Nebenhaus, Richard Swadley, Barbara Mele, and Deirdre Silver.

Frankly, I never expected to be at Wiley for more than twenty years. It's a special place founded in 1807 with family members still actively involved. I got to know Debbie, Peter, and Brad very well. Later on, I also got to work with Jesse. I'm not alone in feeling that I was a part of their family too.

The sales professionals I worked with from Prentice-Hall to Simon & Schuster to Wiley were, quite candidly, the best in the business. We had some record sales years, a lot of fun, and they taught me more than they ever realized. If you enable exceptional people to do their jobs, some pretty remarkable results can occur. I wish there was room here to list the hundreds of salespeople from around the world with whom I've worked. I owe you so much gratitude and I treasure the friendships I have with you all.

Over the course of my publishing career, I've presented and sold to every type of retailer and wholesaler. There are too many to mention them all, but I'm thankful to the brilliant book people at stores and wholesalers like San Diego Technical Books, Borders, the original Joseph Beth Booksellers, Barnes & Noble, Kroch's & Brentano's, Tattered Cover, Book Passage, Baker & Taylor, Amazon, Brown Bookshop of Houston, Advanced Marketing Services, Ingram, Complete Book & Media Supply, and 800CEO Read. I'm grateful to them all.

In early 2016, I read an article on LinkedIn written by Kathe Sweeney. It was very insightful, and I left a comment telling her it was so well done and provided great advice. Kathe and I had been colleagues at one point, but I hadn't spoken directly to her in a while. She was now working at Lynda.com (now LinkedIn Learning) and thanked me for my feedback. It also prompted her to discuss with me the possibility of creating a course or two for sales professionals based on my approach. Now, more than ten courses later, this experience has been so amazing and fun for me. I've thanked Kathe directly in private, but these words will serve as more public recognition of what she has meant to me.

I wrote an article on LinkedIn about the importance of corporate culture and referred to people I've met at Lynda and LinkedIn. What a team and what an amazing company, from the people who handle post-production work to the lighting crew and from the Carpinteria support staff to the makeup people, I've seen firsthand how special and genuine they all are. Along with Kathe, I've worked with really smart, talented, and fun content managers, producers, and directors. Thank you to Susan Williams, Scott Milrad, Lauren Habib, Courtney Brush, Samantha Calamari, Todd Howard, Josh Figatner, Zach Bobbitt, Tony Cruz, Cody Jones, Scott Erickson, Jacob Cunningham, Dathan Graham, Carlos Alfaro, Rob Reich, Jolie Miller, Mordy Golding, Trafford Judd, Doug Winnie, Jeannine Kirk, and Kyle Poll.

Writing this book was an easier process than I had expected. Thankfully, I was fortunate to have worked with Debra Englander who helped edit, provide some structure, and make my thoughts more coherent. She and I had worked together for many years at Wiley, so reconnecting with this book has been great. Debby's editorial and publishing guidance has been invaluable in this entire process.

Throughout my career, I have always told the teams I have managed that family comes first. Our companies will survive if we leave work early to attend a school event, a little league game, or to tend to an ill family member. I've had great and supportive role models in Donna and Peter Holden, Ruthie and Doug Karrel, and Marcia and Robert Dattoli. Each of them clearly understands the importance of family.

This book is dedicated to my children, Melissa and Scott, who have grown up to be terrific individuals. They have each developed in their own careers, but clearly have their priorities focused on the right things in life. To say that I am blessed is an understatement.

Of course, my other dedication goes to my wife, Debbie. She is a cancer survivor with a love of life, laughter, and friendship. Tennis and tap-dancing classes keep her busy but she also volunteers at Teaneck's Holy Name Hospital in a cancer wing, sharing her humor and compassion. She has an amazing ability to talk and relate to virtually anyone and that quality is so helpful to the patients she meets.

ABOUT THE AUTHOR

Dean is an Executive and a Certified Professional Career Coach. He has his own consulting business that provides sales training programs along with motivational and business skills key note presentations. *theskyridgegroup.com*

He is the instructor of more than ten sales related courses available on LinkedIn Learning. They have been viewed more than six hundred thousand times from learners based around the world.

https://www.linkedin.com/learning/instructors/dean-karrel

Dean has been in sales management and leadership positions for more than three decades with major global publishing companies. Most recently, he was Senior Vice President of Sales of Wiley in Hoboken, New Jersey.

Follow Dean on LinkedIn:
https://www.linkedin.com/in/deankarrel/